LEADERS IN THE LORDS:
Government Management and Party Organization
in the Upper Chamber, 1765–1902

LEADERS IN THE LORDS:

Government Management and Party Organization in the Upper Chamber, 1765–1902

Edited by
RICHARD W. DAVIS
Washington University, St Louis

Edinburgh University Press
for
The Parliamentary History Yearbook Trust

© 2003 Edinburgh University Press Ltd

Edinburgh University Press Ltd
22 George Square
Edinburgh

Typeset in Bembo and printed and bound in
Great Britain by Page Bros Ltd, Norwich

A CIP record for this title is available from the British Library

ISBN 0 7486 1835 X

CONTENTS

Preface	vii
RICHARD W. DAVIS, Introduction	1
STEPHEN FARRELL, The Practices and Purposes of Party Leadership: Rockingham and the Lords, 1765–82	13
MICHAEL W. MCCAHILL, William, First Lord Grenville	29
RICHARD W. DAVIS, Wellington	43
JOHN POWELL, The Third Marquess of Lansdowne	57
ANGUS HAWKINS, 'A Host in Himself': Lord Derby and Aristocratic Leadership	75
PETER MARSH, Salisbury's Definition of the Powers of the Lords	91
Index	101

PREFACE

This present collection of essays on *Leadership in the Lords. Government Management and Party Organization in the Upper Chamber, 1765–1902* is the ninth in a series of special volumes sponsored by the journal *Parliamentary History*, and published by Edinburgh University Press for The Parliamentary History Yearbook Trust.

The series consists of volumes on particular topics (like the present one) as well as collections of essays covering specific periods. The tenth in the series to be published in 2004 will be on medieval parliaments in England. Further volumes are planned, including ones on parliament and dissent, parliament and the press, and parliament and print.

In the footnotes the place of publication is London unless otherwise stated.

As editor of *Parliamentary History* I would like to thank the guest editor, Richard Davis, the contributors, and Alasdair Hawkyard who compiled the index.

Clyve Jones
General Editor

LIST OF CONTRIBUTORS

Richard W. Davis, professor of history and director of the Center for the History of Freedom at Washington University in St Louis, edited *Lords of Parliament. Studies, 1714–1914* (Stanford, 1995). He has also written on the house of lords in the Restoration period as well as several books on various aspects of nineteenth-century political and religious history.

Stephen Farrell completed his Cambridge Ph.D. thesis on 'The Rockingham Whig Party and the House of Lords, 1760–85', in 1993, and intends to write his own short study of the eighteenth-century upper chamber. He is currently employed as a senior research office at the History of Parliament, working on the house of commons, 1820–32, with special reference to the Irish M.P.s and constituencies.

Angus Hawkins is a member of the modern history faculty at the University of Oxford and director of international programmes in the Oxford University Department for Continuing Education. His publications include *Parliament, Party and the Art of Politics in Britain, 1855–1859* (1987), *British Party Politics, 1852–1886* (1997), and *Lord Kimberley's Journal, 1862–1902* (1997), co-edited with John Powell, as well as several articles. He is currently completing a political biography of the 14th earl of Derby.

Peter T. Marsh honorary professor of history at the University of Birmingham, is the author of several books that touch on or deal substantially with the 3rd marquess of Salisbury's leadership of the house of lords, including *The Victorian Church in Decline. Archbishop Tait and the Church of England, 1868–1882* (1969), *The Discipline of Popular Government. Lord Salisbury's Domestic Statecraft, 1881–1902* (Hassocks, Sussex, 1978), and *Joseph Chamberlain. Entrepreneur in Politics* (1994).

Michael McCahill is an instructor in history and director of the Robert Lehman Art Center at Brooks School in North Andover, Massachusetts. He is working to complete a study of the house of lords during the reign of George III.

John Powell is associate professor of history at Cumberland College. He is currently investigating the relationship between aristocratic influence and party identification among younger peers in the emerging Liberal party of the mid-Victorian period. His recent books include *Biographical Dictionary of Literary Influences. The Nineteenth Century, 1800–1914* (Westport, Conn., 2001); an edition of *The Journal of John Wodehouse, First Earl of Kimberley, for 1862–1902* (1997), with Angus Hawkins; and John Morley's *On Compromise* (Keele, 1997).

Leaders in the Lords

RICHARD W. DAVIS

The question of when to begin and end any volume on the house of lords in the modern period is not an easy one. It seems that there is hardly a practice or convention of which some previous example cannot be found. And there might not be any more agreement on how large a clump of apparent innovations is enough to signify a significant shift in the institution as a whole. A volume dealing with leadership in the Lords is not immune from such problems.

We have decided to start with the second marquess of Rockingham and to end with the third marquess of Salisbury, that is to span a period from 1765 to 1902. Technically, Rockingham would come under Sir John Sainty's specifications for the official position of leader of the house of lords. He was a prime minister who sat in the Lords; and there can be little doubt that, had his health permitted, he would have led it in his second ministry.[1] No one, however, would contend that Rockingham was the greatest leader of the Lords in the official sense in the eighteenth century. The duke of Newcastle before as well as Lord Grenville after him, for example, both surpassed Rockingham in that capacity. We, however, have used the term leader in a looser sense; for though all the other peers included in the volume did hold the official office, we have not confined our examination to the periods of their tenure alone, and have been concerned as well with their roles as leaders of their parties in the Lords. It is the question of party which justifies beginning with Rockingham; for it was party which began to transform parliamentary politics in his lifetime, in the Lords as well as in the Commons, and which would transform them completely in the following century. Rockingham was a central figure in this transformation, a question to which Stephen Farrell gives a great deal of attention in his essay. Grenville too had an important impact on party, in his case also, perhaps oddly, on the whig party; for it was in the whig party that probably the best of his young men—Lords Althorp, Ebrington, and others—remained after he himself had left, perpetuating principles of both religious and economic liberty of which Grenville was the most likely source.[2] Rockingham and Grenville (who was also, as Michael McCahill shows, the fundamental influence in shaping the official position of leader of the House) prepared the way for Wellington, Lansdowne, Derby and Salisbury, all of whom proved themselves politicians and party leaders of the first order. Such an array of

[1] J. C. Sainty, *Leaders and Whips in the House of Lords, 1783–1964* (House of Lords Record Office Memorandum No. 31, 1964), pp. 1–2. See also the same author's, 'The Origin of the Leadership of the House of Lords', *Bulletin of the Institute of Historical Research*, XLVII (1974).

[2] For the individuals involved, see J. J. Sack, *The Grenvillites, 1801–29* (1979), pp. 166–9. See also, R. W. Davis, 'The House of Lords, the Whigs and Catholic Emancipation 1806–1829', *Parliamentary History*, XVIII (1999), 32.

brilliance and success will perhaps suggest why we decided to end the volume in 1902. For it was not long from the Lords' triumphs over Gladstone under Salisbury's direction to their ignominious defeat by Asquith and Lloyd George in 1911. That that defeat begins a new chapter in the history of the house of lords will not be contested. How much it had to do with faults in the leadership of the then leader of the conservative majority in the Lords, the fifth marquess of Lansdowne, remains to be seen, when scholars have had time to examine fully his papers recently acquired by the British Library. Whatever the conclusion, it is not one that need concern historians of the previous period. For the behaviour of the Lords and their leaders in 1909 to 1911, as well as their spectacular lack of success, marks them off from their nineteenth century predecessors. The Lords between 1765 and 1902 underwent some important changes and suffered some vicissitudes, but none so fundamental as the Parliament Act.

The history of the house of lords in the period has never been extensively studied, and for the last half century and more has been largely ignored.[3] When it has been treated, it has usually been grossly over-simplified, not to say caricatured. There have been two main approaches. One is to see the Lords as primarily the organ of the aristocratic landed classes. The other is to view the upper House as no more than an adjunct of the Conservative party, on the lines of Mr Balfour's poodle. There is obviously some truth in both of these approaches, though neither one nor the other, or both together, provide an adequate explanation of the Lords' behaviour in the nineteenth century. When other explanations fail, when the Lords seem to act neither from self-interest nor from Conservative partisanship, recourse is usually had to a third explanatory device, what we might call the retreat theory. As the name suggests, the theory is based on the assumption that throughout the century, the Lords were in retreat. And it stems from the interpretation of an event when the Lords did retreat, over the passing of the Reform Act of 1832. Then they were forced to give way, and are usually held to have been the great victim of the Reform Act, sustaining a blow to their position in the constitution from which they never recovered.

This was simply not the case. Before 1832, though never merely its tool, the Lords usually deferred to the crown.[4] After 1832 the upper House generally deferred to public opinion. The year 1832, however, was not the crucial turning point. Though there are even earlier examples, the important one for present purposes was in 1828. Then the duke of Wellington explained the Lords' decision to pass the repeal of the Test and Corporation Acts on the grounds that the upper House could not stand in the face of a house of commons backed by public opinion. Putting the explanation in the mouths of the bishops, he said: 'As public men they felt for the consequences of a difference of opinion between the two houses on a question on which the House

---

[3] There are some significant exceptions: M. W. McCahill's pioneering *Order and Equipoise. The Peerage and the House of Lords, 1783–1806* (1978); a brief study by E. A. Smith, *The House of Lords in British Politics and Society, 1815–1911* (1922); and Andrew Adonis, *Making Aristocracy Work. The Peerage and the Political System in Britain, 1884–1914* (Oxford, 1993). *Lords of Parliament. Studies, 1714–1914* (Stanford, CA, 1995), ed. R. W. Davis, contains some useful essays. Significant articles are mentioned in other footnotes.

[4] This was the case right up into the 1820s, even after the practical attraction of patronage had largely disappeared. See D. Large, 'The Decline of "the Party of the Crown" and the Rise of Parties in the Lords, 1783–1837', *English Historical Review*, LXXVIII (1963), 669–95.

of Commons would have been supported by the public opinion.' Clearly methods of determining public opinion in the nineteenth century were rather more haphazard than they are today, and even contemporary politicians sometimes believed they had erred in their assessments of it. In 1834 Wellington stated his conviction that the opinion 'which for the last fifty years has been allowed to have such weight in public councils, I mean public opinion' had actually been that of what he called 'the party in opposition to the government, ... the Dissenters', or at least they had been on the winning side of every question. The duke and other politicians of the time relied on several sources in determining public opinion. In 1828 it is evident that what weighed most heavily with Wellington was some 2,000 petitions. Another indicator was the result of parliamentary elections, especially if these revealed a consistency of sentiment over time; this factor would be particularly important for catholic emancipation, as will be seen presently. In Wellington's case and very likely others, his mailbag, bulging with correspondence from all over the country was still another source. The press was an important factor throughout the nineteenth century.[5]

In 1834 the duke lamented that, unlike the dissenters, the conservative supporters of the Church had thus far not been accustomed to take notice of important questions 'in the way in which we have known them to be noticed by the public'. What he meant was that the conservatives had not advanced their causes by vigorous public agitations. Vigorous agitation was certainly not what Wellington wanted, but he hoped that conservatives would find ways to make their opinions felt. The strong petitioning campaign in favour of the Church in the same year and the general election of 1835 provided a quick answer to those hopes.[6]

In any case, Wellington and his successors continued to honour the principle that the upper House must give way to a house of commons backed by public opinion, and thus in a special way to associate themselves with public opinion. Salisbury took this tendency furthest, and gave it a positive twist, in his referendal theory, which held that if there were any doubt about public opinion on any important government legislation, it was the duty of the Lords to make sure that the issue was referred to the electorate.[7] Wellington did not carry his ideas so far, but the germ was there. Wellington's notions had been developed during the Liverpool government's prolonged agonizing over the catholic emancipation issue. With one exception in 1819, when an emancipation bill failed by only two votes, every house of commons elected after 1812 passed at least one bill, only to have it rejected by the Lords. Peel told the king in 1829 that 'the evil of continued division between two branches of the Legislature on a great constitutional question' which had lasted for 16 years could not go on.[8] Liverpool had in principle been of the same opinion, though he could never bring himself to act on it.

[5] *Lords of Parliament*, ed. Davis, pp. 98, 102; Davis, 'Lords, the Whigs and Catholic Emancipation', pp. 23, 40; Shaun Durham, 'The Duke of Wellington and Public Opinion: A New Dimension', a paper given at the meeting of the Southern Conference on British Studies, Fort Worth, Texas, Nov. 1999.

[6] *Lords of Parliament*, ed. Davis, pp. 102–3.

[7] Corinne Comstock Weston, *The House of Lords and Ideological Politics. Lord Salisbury's Referendal Theory and the Conservative Party, 1846–1922* (Philadelphia, 1995). We are not required to believe that Salisbury himself took this position entirely seriously to accept that it was politically a very useful one.

[8] *Lords of Parliament*, ed. Davis, p. 98.

It may seem puzzling why, if Wellington and the Lords had decided to change their ways and to yield to a house of commons backed by public opinion, they apparently failed, until coerced, to yield in 1831–2. A letter from Wellington to the marquess of Bath at the end of September 1831, just before the Lords' rejection of the Reform Bill on its second reading explains the reason:

> We ... think that there is a very prevailing change of opinion in the country upon the subject of the Bill. At all events we think the House of Lords ought to give the country a chance of being saved by affording further time to consider the question, [and] that in taking this course the House will perform its peculiar function and fulfill its duty in the Constitution.[9]

In short, it was the duty of the Lords not to give way before a sudden upsurge of public opinion, but to be sure that the public had settled on an issue before concurring. In the autumn of 1831, Wellington and other tory leaders were relying on a successful by-election, and other apparently hopeful signs,[10] which clearly did not provide a reliable guide to broader public opinion.

As for May 1832, neither the duke nor apparently the tory lords were prepared to resist the public demand for reform as such. On 28 April, a week before a crisis was precipitated by a tory proposal that a vote on the disfranchising clauses be postponed, Wellington wrote to a clerical confidant that it appeared to him 'quite clear' that: 'We shall have a reform of Parliament on the principle of the bill, either by means of, or without, a creation of peers, according as the King may have firmness to resist and to support those who will insist upon terms for himself, his crown and his country.' After the whig government had resigned, following the king's refusal to create peers, and Wellington had agreed to undertake the royal commission to form a government, there were three large meetings of tory peers at Apsley House. At the first they were informed that '*the king must have reform to a considerable extent.*' At another larger meeting the second day, all but five peers present agreed to give their complete and unqualified adherence to Wellington. At the last meeting on 12 May one of the five, the duke of Newcastle, asked if there was no possibility that the king would be willing to yield a little. Wellington replied, 'no, that it could not be done; the King was already pledged; he had seen the papers and the King was deeply pledged'. The duke of Newcastle was much disturbed, but he gives no indication that any other peer was.[11] To argue that Wellington's leadership throughout the reform controversies of 1830–2 could properly be characterized as mainly moderate, judicious, and skillful would not be easy. What does seem to be evident is that he never believed that he or the Lords could block a reform of parliament on which the public had apparently set its heart. The whig return to office and the passage of the bill only by a massive abstention of its opponents led by Wellington, in order to avoid a creation of peers, certainly appeared to be a massive defeat for the Lords. It also suggested that what had

---

[9] *Ibid.*, p. 99.

[10] Michael Brock, *The Great Reform Act* (1973), pp. 242–3.

[11] *Despatches, Correspondence and Memoranda of Field Marshall Arthur, Duke of Wellington, K.G.* ed. by his son the duke of Wellington (8 vols, 1867–80), VII, 288–9: Wellington to the Rev. G. R. Gleig, 28 Apr. 1832; Nottingham U.L., Newcastle diary, NE 2F/4/1, pp. 116–20. Underlining in the original.

been done once might be done again. So much is true, but that this had any practical effect on the powers of the Lords was not the case.

In the first session of the reformed parliament in 1833, not only did the Lords modify the terms of the abolition of slavery in the colonies in the interests of the West Indian planters, they also rid the whigs' Irish Church Bill of its lay appropriation clause. In 1834 they threw out three major bills, one for Jewish emancipation, another to admit non-anglicans to Oxford and Cambridge, and an Irish Tithe Bill. In 1836 they emasculated another Irish Tithe Bill of its appropriation clause thus forcing the whigs to drop both the bill and the principle thereafter – the principle they had declared as essential and on this issue forced Peel's brief government from office in 1835. Irish poor law legislation introduced in the same year was held up by the Lords for two years, until they found a bill acceptable in 1838. The whigs' other major piece of Irish legislation, a local government measure, had to wait even longer until, much amended, it was finally passed in 1840.

It has been suggested by Leslie Mitchell that this resurgence of the Lords was a fluke, a mere flash in the pan, made possible only because of the whig government's insecure majorities in the Commons during these years. He goes on to quote one of Wellington's numerous deeply pessimistic statements after the passage of the Reform Bill that the house of lords no longer counted for anything. 'Again and again', Mitchell concludes, 'the Lords retreated: over Catholic Emancipation, over Parliamentary Reform and the Corn Laws, and in the face of Mr Lloyd George.'[12]

Dr Mitchell is simply re-stating positions long held by most historians, but they are positions that need re-examination. In the first place, what does it mean to say that 'the Lords retreated'? The picture evoked is obviously that of a vanquished army withdrawing from the field of battle in more or less disarray, but still *one* army. But, whatever else it was, the house of lords was not a single and monolithic force. There were at least two and sometimes more 'armies', and not all of them would have felt vanquished. Indeed those in the majority would have been much more likely to have felt victorious.

As I have shown elsewhere, the reason for the pessimism of the opponents of catholic emancipation and the optimism of its supporters in the last decade of its agitation was the fact that after 1819 the natural tendency among peers (as opposed to bishops) was to support the cause, a tendency which had to be countered by creations. Whatever the reasons for the conversions to the cause, they are very unlikely to have been self-interested ones, since both the king and the prime minister for most of the decade were on the other side. The 89 whig lords who voted for the catholic cause in 1829 certainly felt a thrill of victory for a principle long held; but the 124 tory lords who constituted the largest single group voting for the bill probably did not include many who felt defeated. The 98 ultras who voted against the measure certainly did, but a minority cannot be made the measure of the whole.[13]

As suggested above, 'retreat' seems appropriate enough for 1832. For though neither Wellington nor most of his party were as inflexible on reform or as insensitive to public opinion as has often been thought, much less had any intention of expiring

---

[12] L. G. Mitchell, review of *Lords of Parliament*, E.H.R., CXII (1997), 787.
[13] Davis, 'Lords, Whigs and Catholic Emancipation', pp. 33–43.

in the last ditch, they deeply disliked the Reform Bill and allowed themselves to be manoeuvred into a position where they appeared to be coerced, which is what counted.

As for 1911, I am quite prepared to call that a retreat. The corn laws are a different matter. It was on this question that a famous historian produced a memorable epigram which bears much of the responsibility for the long life of the 'retreat' theory. Of the passage of the repeal measure in the Lords, Elie Halevy observed: 'In 1832 the nobility had sacrificed much of its political to save its economic privileges. Now it sacrificed the most valuable of the latter to save what the Reform Act had left of the former.'[14] Eminent though the source, and elegant the phrases, the content is dubious in every respect.

To take the political aspect first. Writing to the earl of Roden early in the 1833 session, Wellington called 'the House of Lords, an assembly still powerful in legislation; but without political influence'. The statements might seem contradictory, but what Wellington meant by political influence was the power of individual lords to influence the return of members of the house of commons, which was supposed to maintain amity between the two Houses by keeping the Commons generally in agreement with the positions of the Lords.[15] Had such a system of influence been working, it would be hard to understand how it was that the two Houses remained divided for 16 years, over four elections, on catholic emancipation, the single most important political issue of the day; and this, of course, occurred before the Reform Act. Whether the system had ever been as perfect in practice as it was in theory may be doubted; but what is true is that the reduction of aristocratic influence in elections had begun before there was ever a Reform Act, and that the act of 1832 carried the process much further.[16] Historians have laid great stress on the peers' loss of electoral power, and in certain senses quite rightly so: the power of the British nobility was thereby diminished, as it would be later by the decline of its relative economic power. It does not, however, follow that the power of the house of lords ever has been in essence simply a reflection of the sum of the political and economic power of the peerage. While one doubtless affects the other, they remain two different things. Were this not so, the house of lords would have quietly faded into oblivion long ago. As Wellington observed in a memorandum to Lord Lyndhurst in 1835, while deprived of what he called their political influence: 'the House of Lords still constitutionally possesses great power over the legislation of the country in the exercise of which it will be supported by the country; and which it ought to exercise with diligence, with wisdom, and discretion'.[17]

Simply put, Wellington argued, and rightly, that the legislative power of the Lords depended on the country's continued recognition of the legitimacy of that power. He also recognized that the Lords must exercise their power responsibly and must not think that if they did not do so 'this power will be left in the hands of the Peers in

---

[14] Elie Halevy, *A History of the English People in the Nineteenth Century* (6 vols, 1st paperback edn, 1961), IV, 136.

[15] *Lords of Parliament*, ed. Davis, p. 100 and n.

[16] On the latter point, see Ellis Wasson, *Born to Rule. British Political Elites* (Stroud, 2000), pp. 149–58.

[17] Southampton University Library, Wellington papers, WP2/33/78–9.

that they will be able to exercise it with independence (in other words that they will not be swamped)'.[18] The threat of being 'swamped', by the creation of new peers, was one that the duke used occasionally, but less and less as the decade wore on. Nor did the behaviour of the Lords after 1832 suggest that they were trembling at the prospect – a much greater danger was that the whig government would resign before a conservative government was capable of taking its place. The 1832 precedent does not seem to have been a significant restraint on the Lords for long.

As Norman Gash dryly observed in 1965, Halevy's argument about the Lords and the repeal of the corn law 'fits rather awkwardly the role played by the peers since 1832'.[19] They had hardly acted as if they had been shorn of their political power, quite the contrary. Not surprisingly they were less obstreperous after 1841, when Peel's Conservative government came to power. Even the debates over the repeal of the corn laws were remarkably civil; but in the crucial vote 146 Conservative lords voted against the government, about 60 per cent of the party in the Lords. The majority for repeal, however, was not far from being equally divided, with the 96 Conservatives accounting for 46 per cent of the vote.

Who, then, had retreated? Not presumably the 113 whigs, who knew their party was on the way to office. As for the Conservatives, a rough preliminary survey suggests that, for the most part, either their estates lay outside the main corn-growing areas or that their wealth was not primarily dependent on agriculture.[20] This would tend to confirm Professor Gash's informed speculations in 1965. Wellington himself told the duke of Beaufort in December 1845 that he had always hoped that, protected by the corn laws, 'agriculture would become so improved ... that the law might be repealed without injury to any party or to the general interests'. He had been following his own advice for a number of years on his Hampshire estate.[21] How typical the duke was in this respect is difficult to say. It would appear however that most of the conservatives who supported him had, like himself, no crucial economic interest in the corn laws.

In parliament, the duke confined himself to broad constitutional and political arguments. He told the Lords that the bill came to them recommended in the speech from the throne and passed by the house of commons. Without the support of the executive or the other house of parliament, the Lords could do nothing. And as no Conservative was willing to form a government to support the existing corn laws the situation would not change. Neither would the issue go away. Scoffing at the idea that if the Lords could force a dissolution, the protectionists would win the election, he advised that the only thing that further resistance could bring was increasing unrest in the country.[22] It seems likely that many who followed him would have paid attention

---

[18] *Ibid.* Parenthesis in the original.

[19] Norman Gash, *Reaction and Reconstruction in English Politics, 1832–1852* (Oxford, 1965), pp. 47–8.

[20] A systematic study of the question by Professor Iain McLean is under way at Nuffield College, Oxford.

[21] Southampton U.L., WP2/135/17-20; Gash, *Reaction and Reconstruction*, p. 49, n. 2.

[22] The words Wellington used in describing the Lords' position were: 'Without the House of Commons and the Crown, the House of Lords can do nothing.' Halevy suggests that this was meant to convey that they were in a more dire situation than they had been in 1832 (*History of the English People*, IV, 135–6 and n.). The Lords opposing repeal were in a difficult situation, but it was one inherent in their constitutional position and had nothing to do with the earlier crisis. The repeal bill, as it affected revenue,

to his arguments. Some, like the bishops, who much to the fury of the protectionist lords, voted strongly for repeal may have had other, even loftier, reasons. Whatever the reasons of the loyalists, it seems unlikely that the 'retreat' theory would be very useful in explaining them.

It is true, as Dr Mitchell suggests, that the number and importance of public measures either rejected outright or heavily amended by the Lords in the eight years after 1834 was a record unequalled for the rest of the century. But what is true in prospect is also true in retrospect. No government in the century, before as well as after, was so impeded by the Lords as Lord Melbourne's. Why was this so?

In the first place, seemingly intractable differences between Lords and Commons were a new phenomenon in the period. As has been suggested, before the constitutional reforms of 1828 to 1832 the Lords had generally deferred to the crown. An excellent example is provided by Grayson Ditchfield in his discussion of the issue raised in the 1770s by the requirement that dissenting ministers subscribe to the Thirty-nine Articles of the Church of England. Because of the relative closeness of a general election, in 1772 Lord North's government decided not to oppose in the Commons a dissenting effort to remove the necessity of subscription, but rather to block it in the Lords. The measure therefore easily passed the Commons, only to be overwhelmingly defeated in the Lords, as a result of strenuous efforts by the government leader there, strongly backed by the king. A bill the next year, with modifications to meet some of the Lords' objections, failed by only a slightly smaller margin. In 1779, however, with growing pressures of war in America, Europe and the world, and the need to placate religious minorities, among others, for the sake of the war effort, the government decided that it was inexpedient to oppose the measure, and it easily passed both the Commons and the Lords – in the latter case, the total vote was a mere 19, with only one opposed. Once again, however, there had been modifications to meet the Lords' criticisms. In short, during this earlier period, the Lords were in general agreement with the king's government; when called upon, they were prepared to support it in force; and, so long as decent attention was paid to their opinions, to accommodate themselves to the needs of its shifting policies.[23]

After 1812 things changed. With the declaring of the catholic question an open one, significant divisions on this and other religious questions became apparent, in parliament as well as in the country.[24] Political parties rallied around them, and public opinion (or what passed for it) began to be expressed strongly and regularly. It was these circumstances, with the subsequent addition of other connected issues such as parliamentary reform, that caused the division in parliament into two broad camps; and in the Lords, the tory or conservative camp, was usually reliably larger. It was this situation that caused the great vicissitudes of Melbourne's government.

---

[22] *(continued)* was a money bill and therefore could not be amended by the Lords (Gash, *Reaction and Reconstruction*, p. 51, n. 1). No leading conservative was prepared to form a government to support the principle of the existing law or even on the general principle of protection (Southampton U.L., WP2/134/134-6). Therefore all the Lords could have done was to reject the bill with no immediate prospect of anyone being ready to take up their cause.

[23] G. M. Ditchfield, 'The Subscription Issue in British Parliamentary Politics, 1772–79', *Parliamentary History*, VII (1988), 45–80.

[24] Davis, 'Lords, the Whigs and Catholic Emancipation', pp. 29–30.

It was not a state of affairs that could have gone on forever. But the reason for the change lay not only in large majorities in the lower House. Lord John Russell's government, for example, can hardly be called secure in the house of commons. Nevertheless, the Lords, under the leadership of Lansdowne, passed the repeal of the Navigation Acts in 1849. The reason for the minority status of the government in the Commons and of its success in the Lords is the same. The corn law crisis had broken the Conservative party in two. In the Commons, Russell depended on the good will of the Peelites. In the Lords, however, as Angus Hawkins shows, a more unstable mixture of whigs, Peelites, and Conservatives of both free trade and protectionist persuasions denied Derby for a while his full inheritance from Wellington. In the meantime, Lansdowne had full scope for his great talents of conciliation and coalition building, which John Powell discusses. Yet even when Derby had been largely successful in regrouping the Conservatives in the Lords, he avoided conflict, not out of fear of retribution, but as a matter of deliberate policy, aimed at weakening his opposition by leaving them to fight among themselves.

Derby, however, did not hesitate to put the Lords on the attack when he saw the chance of advantage. If Gladstone's four governments were rolled together, his record of suffering inflicted by the upper House would exceed even Melbourne's. And the conflict began even before he gained the premiership. Seeing the opportunity to exploit and exacerbate differences within the liberal government Derby led the Lords in a successful attack on the chancellor's bill to abolish paper duties in 1860. Gladstone achieved success the next year, by including repeal of the paper duties with other money bills in a single budget, which the Lords could not reject *in toto*. This was clever, which was just as well, as Gladstone was in no position to be masterful. During his first government in 1869, the Lords, admonished by Salisbury, did not attempt to defeat the bill for the disestablishment of the Irish Church, which had just been the major issue in a general election; but they managed to lessen significantly the extent of its disendowment. In 1871 they struck at a key part of Edward Cardwell's proposed military reforms, rejecting the proposal to abolish the sale of commissions in the army, and forcing the government to have recourse to a royal warrant. This was perhaps the sharpest public clash in Gladstone's first government, but the anticipation alone of opposition by the Lords was often enough to prevent its necessity. Colin Matthew says of the proposal for education reform in 1870 drawn up by W. E. Forster and Lord De Grey that Gladstone 'never made any attempt to modify the structure of their plan. This was not surprising as it was the only plan likely to survive the Lords.'[25]

In his second and fourth governments, Gladstone clashed with the new Conservative leader, Lord Salisbury, on public questions of the first importance. As Peter Marsh shows, Salisbury, using the Lords as his chosen instrument and using them with consummate skill, inflicted two signal defeats on the veteran prime minister. In 1884 he managed to block the Reform Bill until he had secured the concession of a Redistribution Bill, thus greatly reducing the liberal advantage that might have accrued if the one had been carried without the other. The 1832 solution of threatening a creation was never seriously considered by the government.[26] In 1893 Salisbury once

---

[25] H. C. G. Matthew, *Gladstone, 1809–1898* (Oxford, 1997), p. 205.
[26] *Ibid.*, p. 430.

again delivered a powerful blow to the liberal prime minister when he led the Lords in an overwhelming rejection of another Irish Home Rule Bill, which embodied Gladstone's final attempt to carry the last great cause of his career. The government saw no alternative but to swallow its defeat.

The last issue suggests the reasons for the Lords' considerable success and influence in nineteenth-century politics. The upper House was blessed with leaders of real talent and judgement, who by and large did not enter contests which they were not confident they could win. This meant that the Lords did not engage in conflicts in which a government loss was likely to mean a dissolution. Irish home rule in 1893 was clearly not such an issue, which was why Salisbury chose it. And the striking conservative successes in the later 1830s were based on a similar calculation. The whig government had seriously underestimated public support for the established Church, which in the case of Irish policy added a further public prejudice against it. These were the kinds of issues Conservatives could fight and win, and they did. On other issues that were obviously popular, such as the abolition of colonial slavery in 1833 and municipal reform in 1835, they might amend bills, but they could not safely oppose them outright. Here the balance could be delicate; in the municipal corporations bill of 1835 Conservative attempts to amend it went too far, and Wellington had to order a withdrawal. Derby's inclination to caution and restraint and giving his opponents plenty of rope to hang themselves also had the result of avoiding any severe conflicts during his long leadership. Salisbury too had a notion of limits, as his opposition to all-out war against the disestablishment of the Irish Church shows. He may have taken risks over the Reform Bill; but they were carefully calculated and the campaign conducted with a brilliance that was the greater for its coolness. He never let the enemy outflank him, and in the end he beat them on their own ground. Salisbury may have been daring, but he was not rash. Those who succeeded him appear to have been.

All the leaders we have surveyed enjoyed marked success. What characteristics did they share that might help explain this success? With the exception of Lansdowne in his later years (when, as John Powell shows, he had younger assistants of a high calibre), all paid close attention to the details of leadership: to summoning lords to parliament; to proxies and their disposition; to lists of supporters and opponents; to movers and seconders of the address. While most or all of the duties involved might usually be left to the whip, this, of course, did not mean that they had not been carefully reviewed by the leader. The clearest example, and greatly to his own benefit in the end, was Wellington, who when the corn law issue deprived him of his whip simply assumed the duties himself. But all the other leaders give evidence of the same sort of attention to detail.

A leader's entertainment of his followers was a mixture of flattery and the imparting of necessary information, and again all the leaders studied were careful not to neglect it. Wellington complained bitterly, but he knuckled under; and as far as meetings mainly for information and consultation went, he surpassed them all. There were probably two reasons for this. One, as will be seen later, was that such meetings served him well. But the demand was also probably greatest in his time, when the tories passed from being a party of government to being an ordinary party, sometimes out of office.

The transition involved new duties for tory leaders in opposition. As Michael McCahill shows, Grenville made himself an expert on the election of Scottish representative peers when he was the official leader of the Lords. And he had much to do with designing an Irish representative peerage intended to avoid some of the inconveniences he saw in the Scottish one. After Wellington took the power of electing Scottish and Irish representative peers with him when he left office in 1830, those elections became another important responsibility of conservative leaders, and they did not neglect it.

Grenville, Lansdowne, Derby and Salisbury gained fame for their powerful oratory in their youth and sustained that fame to their graves. Whatever their special strengths, all could render the most complex subjects apparently lucid and thereby persuade their followers. Neither Rockingham nor Wellington had these talents to the same degree, and thus rather than taking personal charge of introducing legislation in the House, they tended to speak late in debates just before the vote, when they could exhort and put their own imprint on proceedings.

It is doubtless significant that, while the others had all had distinguished careers in the Commons and risen to high office while there, Rockingham had no experience as an M.P. and Wellington not much. The latter's three years in the Commons, two of them as Irish secretary, were interrupted by military service, his talent for which was also part of his attraction for the Irish post. His parliamentary performance had not been markedly successful.

It might be said of Grenville, Lansdowne, Derby and Salisbury that they possessed conventional talents to a remarkable degree. They could sway the House by their rhetoric and use it to guide legislation through. Beyond that, all were masters both of strategy and tactics, as the essays in this volume amply demonstrate. Wellington possessed the latter talents to a superlative degree. And he made up for lack of oratorical skills to a large extent by the infinite pains he took to meet with and persuade his followers.

Similarly, as Stephen Farrell argues, Rockingham's influence with his followers rested in large part on his 'mild captaincy'. He too led with patience, good nature and persuasion. His career was in many ways a tragic one. He was prime minister twice, once when he was too inexperienced to enjoy the full power of the office and the next time when he was dying. But in between, in opposition he led in the creation of a new kind of party which was to transform politics for his successors. He helped to endow his party with distinctive and enduring principles, connected with and reaching out to emerging strands of public opinion. In the house of lords he adapted or devised ways to keep the party's positions before parliament and the country, whether by the traditional means of published protests or by promoting debate on the address at the beginning of the session.

Grenville, as an opposition leader after 1807, would use the Lords in much the same way, as a tribune from which to proclaim party positions. But before that he had largely defined the office of official leader of the House. Between them, Rockingham and Grenville established the clear outlines of the system in which their nineteenth-century successors would work, and work very effectively.

As has been argued earlier, the house of lords as an institution was certainly no less powerful after 1832 than before; its power to reject bills sent up from the Commons remained intact. Whether its power was greater depends on several contingent factors and how they are weighted, and cannot be settled here. But a few suggestions are possible. It is generally agreed that in the eighteenth century, the influence of the crown, resting on a solid basis of patronage, was necessary to get the government's business done in both houses of parliament. With the dwindling of the crown's patronage in the late eighteenth and early nineteenth centuries, its influence also dwindled. The rise of party was more or less simultaneous with these latter developments, and in time party organization helped supply the need created by the decline of royal influence.

It may well be that in the eighteenth century and the first couple of decades of the nineteenth the Lords' willingness to accommodate itself to the wishes of the crown depended more on genuine agreement on broad principles of government than on either the carrot or the stick of patronage. At the same time, agreement in principle is one thing, getting out and acting on it is another; and here, in organizing the Lords for action, the lure of patronage and honours was of critical importance.

Did parties and party discipline prove entirely sufficient to their purpose? As Angus Hawkins, the leading authority on party in the nineteenth century, reminds us, parties in the Lords were primarily voluntary alliances, based on friendship and common principles. The Lords were not elected and there were not enough offices and honours to go very far in the building of majorities. There was no basis here for stringent party discipline. It seems reasonable to conclude, then, that individual lords were freer of any sort of predominating influence in the nineteenth than they had been in the eighteenth century.

Would this have made the institution stronger or weaker? It can be argued that it made it stronger. It was the gradual conversion of individual peers to catholic emancipation that convinced Liverpool and Wellington that the bastion was crumbling beneath them, and that it could not hold out much longer. And it would appear to have been a similar sort of process that allowed Wellington to produce from his own party only a little under half of the votes in the Lords that repealed the corn laws. The looseness of party discipline provided the house of lords with a greater flexibility in adjusting to new issues and situations than it would otherwise have had. Would inflexibility have been a sign or source of greater strength? It is doubtful.

The sanction the Lords respected was, as has been suggested, public opinion. But the state of public opinion at any given time was not always apparent. To keep in line with it, or at any rate to avoid antagonizing it, required leaders of great intelligence and unusual judgement. By and large, most of the time, the Lords enjoyed such leadership in the nineteenth century.

The Practices and Purposes of Party Leadership: Rockingham and the Lords, 1765–82[*]

STEPHEN FARRELL

Charles Watson–Wentworth, second marquess of Rockingham, was an unlikely choice for the parliamentary leadership of the small number of opposition whig M.P.s and peers who together formed a distinct and unique political party in the third quarter of the eighteenth century. The role was thrust upon him from the time that he became prime minister in July 1765, although it was not at first clear that he would be the undisputed head of this coalition government or that the duke of Newcastle's recently dispossessed corps would continue to remain separate from the court whig majority. So it would be more accurate to date his ascendancy over his reduced group of friends, later known as the Rockingham whig party, from the year after his loss of office in July 1766. From then onwards his authority, for all its evident limitations, was never directly challenged, even by his more exasperated supporters, up until his death, which occurred within a few months of his return to power in 1782.[1] Frank O'Gorman has rightly commented that 'Proceedings in parliament were organized by the characteristically Rockinghamite qualities of personal informality and intermittent enthusiasm',[2] and less sympathetic or well informed judgments have sometimes been passed on Rockingham's managerial shortcomings.[3] Yet it is possible to dispel the impression of vacillation and lack of direction which attended Rockingham's leadership, a period of 16 years in the political wilderness. The questions that should be asked are whether his parliamentary record was really so bad, and how, if his leadership *was* still relatively poor, he nevertheless sought and achieved prominence for himself and his party in national politics?

This article will not only argue that Rockingham's performance deserves a more favourable interpretation, but it will also demonstrate that there was a wider party imperative which helps to explain his parliamentary conduct. In concentrating on Rockingham's role as party leader in the Lords, the following analysis will provide a

---

[*] I wish to express my gratitude to Olive, Countess Fitzwilliam's Wentworth Settlement Trustees and the Director of Sheffield City Libraries for permission to quote from the Rockingham papers; and to Dr G. M. Ditchfield for his comments on a draft of this paper.

[1] For Rockingham's career, see Paul Langford, *The First Rockingham Administration, 1765–1766* (Oxford, 1973); Ross J. S. Hoffman, *The Marquis. A Study of Lord Rockingham, 1730–1782* (New York, 1973); Frank O'Gorman, *The Rise of Party in England. The Rockingham Whigs, 1760–1782* (1975); and Warren M. Elofson, *The Rockingham Connection and the Second Founding of the Whig Party, 1768–1773* (Montreal and Kingston, Ontario, 1996).

[2] Frank O'Gorman, 'Party in the Later Eighteenth Century', in *The Whig Ascendancy. Colloquies on Hanoverian England*, ed. John Cannon (1981), p. 83.

[3] E.g., Arthur Stanley Turberville, *The House of Lords in the XVIIIth Century* (Oxford, 1927), pp. 322–3, 351–2, 401, 491.

brief survey of most of the techniques of parliamentary organization.[4] However, in addition to the practices of political leadership, emphasis will be placed on the purposes of party management in relation to events which *occurred* in the House of Lords, but whose effects *reverberated* beyond the chamber and through the political nation as a whole. Given that his minority party was bound to remain in opposition if it eschewed full co-operation with other political groups, there was an understandable incentive for it sometimes to shift the onus away from the parliamentary arena, where it was unlikely to be able to reverse its unending cycle of defeats. By enlarging the ambit of the party discourse, Rockingham therefore attempted to present a rationale for apparently inexplicable failure, to resort (if only very cautiously) to the court of public opinion and to appeal beyond the mundane routines of parliamentary activity to some universal standard of virtuous consistency. So, as he endeavoured conscientiously to improve his own performance as parliamentary leader, he at the same time sought to break through the barrier of unpopularity which seemed to cordon his party off from so much of the political community. And if he was conscious of how poorly he was rated by his contemporaries, he expected also to be vindicated in the judgment of posterity.

Rockingham's difficulties as leader in the Lords reflected his general character, which was a curious mixture of personal discomfiture in the cauldron of politics and an unquenchable sense of patriotic duty. These problems can be examined within four roughly consecutive periods. During his first spell as prime minister, his inexperience and diffidence meant that he had to undergo a severe apprenticeship in the role and duties of the 'leader' of the Lords. Over the ensuing eight years, the necessity of mounting an effective opposition led him to pursue largely unsuccessful tactics, some of which were well removed from the increasingly forlorn party conflict. From 1770 to 1778 the adverse conditions for opposition forced him to develop a more strategic attitude, in which he attempted to bring the party's stance further into the public domain. Finally, especially in the eight years to 1782, Rockingham had to confront the dilemma of how to highlight his party and his own authority within the growing range of voices arrayed against ministers. Towards the end of his career he headed a party of high, but ultimately unfulfilled, political potential. Yet, across the whole period, it was his ability to represent the overarching ideological principles of his party to a political audience that, for all his foibles in parliament, made his position as party leader so unassailable.[5]

1

Although Rockingham spent most of his leadership in opposition, eventually becoming a reasonably proficient speaker and manager, it was his weak performance

---

[4] For the Lords during this period, see Michael W. McCahill, 'The House of Lords in the 1760s', in *A Pillar of the Constitution. The House of Lords in British Politics, 1640–1784*, ed. Clyve Jones (1989), pp. 165–98; G. M. Ditchfield, 'The House of Lords in the Age of the American Revolution', in *ibid.*, pp. 199–239; and William C. Lowe, 'Politics in the House of Lords, 1760–1775', Emory University Ph.D., 1975. For the eighteenth-century background, see Geoffrey Holmes, *British Politics in the Age of Anne* (rev. edn, 1987), esp. ch. 12; and the articles (and bibliography) in *Peers, Politics and Power. The House of Lords, 1603–1911*, ed. Clyve Jones and David Lewis Jones (1986).

[5] For a detailed account of Rockingham's leadership, see Stephen Farrell, 'Divisions, Debates and "Dis-Ease": The Rockingham Whig Party and the House of Lords, 1760–1785', University of Cambridge Ph.D., 1993, esp. pp. 128–34 and chs. 5–7.

in his first term as prime minister which is usually remembered to his discredit. In particular, his failure to summon up sufficient courage to speak on the address of thanks in December 1765, and again at the real start of the session in January 1766, was an embarrassment which obviously failed to inspire confidence.[6] Of one of the very few occasions that year when he did venture to intervene, explaining to the disgruntled Lords on 20 January why not all the papers relating to the American Stamp Act crisis had been laid, he admitted in his report to George III, that he 'never wished more for the Power of any degree of Oratory than then'.[7] A nervous speaker, who, despite the relatively decorous atmosphere in the Lords, was plainly at a loss when confronted by the combativeness and expertise of the small number of accomplished debaters, he lacked any ministerial experience of handling the House.[8] Despite his intimacy with the older generation of leading opposition whig peers, notably Newcastle, and his enhanced profile among the younger members of the connexion in the Commons,[9] he can hardly be described as the 'whip of whiggery' in the three years to 1765,[10] although he had been involved in procuring the attendance of friends in the Lords.[11]

Over the previous hundred years, there had been several effective government managers in the upper chamber, notably the earls of Danby and Oxford.[12] In addition, the eighteenth century had seen the development of the official position of 'leader' of the Lords, who, if the prime minister sat in the Commons, was the northern or, from the 1760s, the more senior secretary of state.[13] Newcastle, now lord privy seal, had long served as the nominal or effective government 'leader' and so was ideally placed, as well as characteristically eager, to tutor the man whom he regarded as his protégé.[14] Rockingham, who sought his advice on how to arrange peers' attendance at the pre-Christmas eve-of-session meeting, was therefore coached through the process of formulating the king's speech and of choosing the mover and seconder of the address.[15] For both the pre-sessional gatherings, which took place

[6] E.g., Richard Pares, *King George III and the Politicians* (Oxford, 1953), p. 82; Paul Langford, *Public Life and the Propertied Englishman, 1689–1798* (Oxford, 1991), p. 578.

[7] *The Correspondence of King George the Third, From 1760 to December 1783*, ed. Sir John Fortescue (6 vols, 1927), I, 240.

[8] He had only ever held office in the household, as a lord of the bedchamber, 1751–62.

[9] Sir Lewis Namier, *England in the Age of the American Revolution* (2nd edn, 1961), ch. 5; D. H. Watson, 'The Rise of the Opposition at Wildman's Club', *Bulletin of the Institute of Historical Research*, XLIV (1971), 55–77.

[10] Hoffman, *The Marquis*, ch. 2, exaggerates his role here.

[11] E.g., Sheffield City Libraries, Sheffield Archives, Wentworth Woodhouse Muniments [hereafter W.W.M.], Rockingham papers, R1–370: Newcastle to Rockingham, 27 Mar. 1763.

[12] Andrew Swatland, *The House of Lords in the Reign of Charles II* (Cambridge, 1996), pp. 251–3, 263; Clyve Jones, ' "The Scheme Lords, the Neccessitous Lords, and the Scots Lords": The Earl of Oxford's Management and the "Party of the Crown" in the House of Lords, 1711–14', in *Party and Management in Parliament, 1660–1784*, ed. Clyve Jones (Leicester, 1984), p. 143.

[13] John C. Sainty, 'The Origin of the Leadership of the House of Lords', *B.I.H.R.*, XLVII (1974), 57, 59–60; Anita J. Rees, 'The Practice and Procedure of the House of Lords, 1714–1784', University of Wales (Aberystwyth) Ph.D., 1987, pp. 68–9, 250–1. For clarification of the emergence of this role in the 1710s, see Clyve Jones, 'The Origin of the Leadership of the House of Lords Revisited', *Historical Research*, LXXII (1999), 268–84.

[14] Sainty, 'Origin of the Leadership', pp. 59, 68–9.

[15] B.L., Add. MS 32972, ff. 176–7: Rockingham to Newcastle, 9 Dec.; W.W.M., R1–539, 623: Newcastle to Rockingham, 10, [14] Dec. 1765.

at Rockingham's house in Grosvenor Square on 16 December 1765 and 13 January 1766, Rockingham supplied the king with lists of lords present and of 'remarkable absentees'.[16] This provides confirmation that he was personally filling the role of 'leader' while prime minister. However, although he kept George III informed of proceedings in the Lords, in this latter duty he was assisted by the northern secretary, the duke of Grafton,[17] upon whom, as one government supporter later wrote, 'the labouring Oar had lain in the House of Lords'.[18]

As the king's chief minister, Rockingham would normally have enjoyed the direction of what historians have come to call the 'party of the crown', comprising government and household office-holders, Scottish representative peers, bishops and other lords who were in some sense dependent on the court.[19] But because part of George Grenville's cabinet had been retained and William Pitt was looked to as the obvious premier in waiting, Rockingham found that his predominance over this by no means always compliant body of ministerialists was greatly reduced. When the government's controversial policy of repealing the Stamp Act, a measure about which George III was known to have reservations, was discussed in the Lords, the weakness of the administration was revealed, for, in the committee on the Stamp Act papers, ministers were defeated on significant opposition amendments to the fourth and last of their five resolutions (by 63–60 on 4 February and 59–55 on 6 February 1766). Several of the 'king's friends' voted against government and George III refused either to urge the attendance of the more loyal, or to dismiss the more recalcitrant, of them.[20] Not the least of the premier's shortcomings was that his aloof style alienated the monarch and, in general, Rockingham's superficially arrogant manner failed to attract adherents outside his immediate circle. He neglected to appease the Buteites in order to shore up his ministry and never grasped the importance of Newcastle's example of making himself the centre of a large web of contacts and correspondents.[21] Once in opposition, the loss of royal sanction and Rockingham's inattentiveness were to accelerate the attrition of 'natural' courtiers from his connexion.[22]

The underlying weaknesses of the ministry in the upper chamber made it imperative that supporters be gathered in for the second reading of the Stamp Act Repeal Bill, which, with the Declaratory Bill, formed the government's principal legislation. Once passed by the Commons on 4 March 1766, and with the king's stated preference for repeal over enforcement (modification being ruled out), the prospects of success improved in the Lords, where as a financial measure the Repeal Bill could not be

---

[16] 'The House of Lords, 1660–1800: List of Lists', in *British Parliamentary Lists, 1660–1800. A Register*, ed. G. M. Ditchfield, David Hayton and Clyve Jones (1995) [hereafter 'Lords Lists'], nos. 247, 249.

[17] Sainty, 'Origin of the Leadership', pp. 60–1, 69–70.

[18] B.L., Add. MS 35428, f. 26: 2nd earl of Hardwicke's 'Memorial of Family Occurrences', Jan. 1771.

[19] Jones, '"Scheme lords"', p. 123; David C. Large, 'The Decline of the "Party of the Crown" and the Rise of Parties in the House of Lords, 1783–1837', *English Historical Review*, LXXVIII (1963), 669–95.

[20] For the repeal, see also Peter D. G. Thomas, *British Politics and the Stamp Act Crisis. The First Phase of the American Revolution, 1763–1767* (Oxford, 1975), chs 11–12.

[21] Reed Browning, *The Duke of Newcastle* (New Haven, 1975), pp. 77, 83, 86–7, 321; O'Gorman, *Rise of Party*, pp. 118–19.

[22] It is no surprise that almost no members of the 'party of the crown' adhered to the Rockingham whigs after 1766, or that they rarely had a leading lawyer among their parliamentary ranks.

altered, but only approved or defeated. Newcastle produced a long series of surveys,[23] and Rockingham, who had some experience of compiling lists, apparently came in at the end of this process, using various pieces of information to construct at least two others (7 March and undated).[24] Both leaders were highly accurate in their final calculations on the measure, which was committed on 11 March by 105 votes to 71 (including proxies), with 17 absentees.[25] Comparing Rockingham's first forecast, based on the presence list for 7 March, four days before the crucial division, with the actual division list shows that 65 of the 70 he listed as 'supposed for' voted for the bill in person, and 50 of the 54 'supposed agt' were present to vote against it.[26] Thereafter, Rockingham was not assiduous in his use of management lists, although he did construct one on the eve of his second ministry,[27] but with a relatively small and close knit group of about 30 lords, during a period of largely stable political alignments, it was a relatively easy task to keep track of his party's voting strength.[28]

The crisis over the Repeal Bill also brought into focus the necessity for government to ensure its superiority in terms of proxies,[29] and, after a flurry of additions, the Rockingham ministry's majority on 11 March 1766 was raised from 12 to 34 by the lead it had in proxies, of which 32 were given for and 10 against the second reading.[30] In the years of opposition that followed, Rockingham almost invariably held the maximum of two proxies and he entrusted his own to the duke of Richmond during his absences, from illness, during the sessions of 1770–1, 1772 and 1775–6.[31] He clearly made efforts to ensure that most of his supporters left proxies, if they could not attend on important occasions,[32] and, as Newcastle had done, he used the offices of the clerk assistant to help with the technicalities of having them entered.[33] Ministers always dominated the struggle for proxies, which meant that it was sometimes worth trying to force a division in a committee, where they could not be called for.[34] However, by securing and recording in divisions the proctorial representation of his

[23] 'Lords Lists', nos. 256–63.

[24] *Ibid.*, nos. 262, 264. W.W.M., R53 contains several, including earlier, lists in Rockingham's hand. He used R53–21 and 24 ('Lords Lists', nos. 259, 264), an extract from the proxy book (R53-7), and copies of the manuscript minutes (W.W.M., R5).

[25] 'Lords Lists', no. 265.

[26] *Ibid.*, nos. 262, 265; *L.J.*, XXXI, 300-1. Perhaps surprised by the high attendance of 136 lords, he was eight short on his own side and ten on the opposition side. The 11 he listed as 'supposed doubtful' split eight to three against the government.

[27] 'Lords Lists', no. 350.

[28] For the structure of the party, see Stephen Farrell, 'Division Lists and the Nature of the Rockingham Whig Party in the House of Lords, 1760–1785', *Parliamentary History*, XIII (1994), 170–89.

[29] W.W.M., R1–577: Newcastle to Rockingham, 9 Feb. 1766.

[30] Between 10 Feb. and 11 Mar. 1766, an additional 39 proxies were registered, of which 22 had not been voided up to and including 11 Mar., when 15 were placed in favour of the Repeal Bill, with six against (while one proxy-holder was absent): H.L.R.O., Proxy Book, no. 38 (1765); 'Lords Lists', C16.

[31] H.L.R.O., Proxy Books, nos. 38–54 (1765–1781/2).

[32] E.g., W.W.M., R153–10: Rockingham to Burke, 17 May 1775.

[33] B.L., Add. MS 32975, ff. 260-1: Newcastle to Bishop Thomas of Winchester, 24 May 1766; Nottingham U.L., Portland papers, PwF 9095: Rockingham to Portland, 7 Nov. 1775.

[34] Newcastle made this point in advance of a Bedfordite initiative on America, and the government won two divisions by only three votes (65–62) in committee on 26 May 1767: W.W.M., R1–723: Newcastle to Rockingham, 23 May 1767; *The Parliamentary History of England, From the Norman Conquest, in 1066, to the Year 1803*, ed. William Cobbett (36 vols, 1806-20) [hereafter Cobbett], XVI, 360–1.

friends, Rockingham at least prevented the further dilution of the party among those who were inclined to absent themselves from parliament.[35]

2

For a while after 1766 there was little perception that Rockingham, who consolidated his own position as party leader, would remain out of power for a long time. Yet the eight years which followed his return to opposition, during which the struggle for office gradually became more futile, were to be the formative ones for his party, perhaps largely because of its parliamentary disappointments.[36] In the considerable endeavours which Rockingham did make in the Lords, the tactics that he adopted both mimicked those of government and echoed, wittingly or not, the earlier eighteenth-century stratagems of ambitious 'outs' again to become 'ins'.[37] He made little attempt to organize his friends in advance of the 1766–7 session,[38] and their initially sympathetic attitude to the administration of the earl of Chatham (as Pitt had become) prevented any significant contribution to the Grenvillite attack on the corn embargo proclamation in the autumn of 1766.[39] However, in subsequent years, following the usual summer 'conciliabulum' of party leaders at Rockingham's residence of Wentworth Woodhouse in Yorkshire, preparations, if only limited ones, were generally carried out, with supporters being summoned and meetings held before the start of the session.[40] Rockinghamite attacks were occasionally made on the address,[41] and in other respects, too, the whigs – including Rockingham – squared up to the ministries of Chatham and Grafton, increasingly involving themselves in the uninspiring minutiae of parliamentary opposition.[42]

This, however, would not have been sufficient to force a change of government and therefore Rockingham on several occasions co-operated with the other significant elements in opposition. The most spectacular example of such an alliance occurred in mid-1767, when, after a damaging split within their own ranks on 10 April,[43] the Rockinghams acted with the groups led by Grenville and the duke of Bedford in a concerted and very nearly victorious campaign in the Lords. As agreed at various

---

[35] But see Ditchfield, 'Lords in the Age of the American Revolution', p. 229.

[36] Most authorities place the formation of the Rockingham whig party in the years 1766–8: e.g., John Brooke, *The Chatham Administration, 1766–1768* (1956), p. 291. But see Warren M. Elofson, 'The Rockingham Whigs in Transition: The East India Company Issue, 1772–1773', *E.H.R.*, CIV (1989), 947–74.

[37] Clyve Jones, 'The House of Lords and the Growth of Parliamentary Stability, 1701–1742', in *Britain in the First Age of Party, 1680–1750. Essays Presented to Geoffrey Holmes*, ed. Clyve Jones (1987), pp. 85–110 (esp. pp. 102–5); Ditchfield, 'Lords in the Age of the American Revolution', pp. 200–2, 232–3.

[38] Nottingham U.L., Portland papers, PwF 7526: Newcastle to Portland, 7 Nov. 1766.

[39] Philip Lawson, 'Parliament, the Constitution and Corn: The Embargo Crisis of 1766', *Parliamentary History*, V (1986), 17–37.

[40] H.M.C., *14th Report, Appendix, Part X*, pp. 57, 68, 74: Rockingham to Dartmouth, 15 Aug. 1767, 8 Nov. 1769, 12 Nov. 1770; Ditchfield, 'Lords in the Age of the American Revolution', p. 228.

[41] E.g., at the start of the 1770–1 session: W.W.M., R1–1326: Rockingham to Chatham, 15 Nov. 1770.

[42] E.g., *Proceedings and Debates of the British Parliaments Respecting North America, 1754–1783*, ed. R. C. Simmons and Peter D. G. Thomas (6 vols, Millwood and White Plains, 1982–7), III, 252.

[43] *The Correspondence of Edmund Burke*, ed. Thomas Copeland *et al.* (10 vols, Cambridge, 1958–70) [hereafter *Burke Correspondence*], I, 308: Burke to O'Hara, [18 Apr. 1767].

private meetings, they used a range of sophisticated techniques: posing questions to the judges on the powers of the American colonies (on 22 and 26 May);[44] moving an address to the crown on the government of Quebec (on 2 June);[45] and securing papers and examining witnesses on the financial state of the East India Company (for example, on 25 June).[46] According to the usually hostile commentator Horace Walpole, 'In such manoeuvres [the active Bedford whigs Lord] Sandwich and [M.P. Richard] Rigby were excellent; and Lord Rockingham himself, who had been so indolent a minister, was become as industrious a partizan as either of them'.[47] The junction was short-lived, as were the abortive attempts at united action taken with Chatham's small clique in 1770 and 1771, so that, even in potentially advantageous circumstances, the voting strength and procedural forces were stacked against opposition in parliament.[48] However, while the failure of such lively initiatives marked the relegation of the party to the outlying margins of politics, it also produced a certain uniformity of ideological and psychological outlook, which strengthened Rockingham's hold over the corps.[49]

That authority extended equally to the party's M.P.s, who, after the general election of 1768, numbered 54, with Rockingham, who returned no fewer than ten of them, being the greatest of his group's electoral patrons.[50] Co-ordination between the party's members in both chambers was particularly sensitive on issues affecting the powers of the Commons. In the aftermath of the Portland-Lowther affair over the Cumberland contest and perhaps emboldened by his recent interventions on another area of predominantly Commons (and royal) concern, the civil list, Rockingham supervised the passage of the Nullum Tempus Bill in March 1769, an example of how he could sometimes secure the passage of minor legislation.[51] At an institutional level, an official conference between managers from the two Houses could be used to smooth over differences, and in Rockingham's absence, Richmond unsuccessfully attempted to employ this tactic on the East India Company Restraining and Regulation Bills, on 21 December 1772 and 11 June 1773 respectively.[52] A more regular practice was to introduce identical motions in each House on the same day as, for instance, on the crisis over the Falkland Islands on 22 November 1770; it was during the furore over this issue, that Rockingham (among other peers) was expelled from the Commons the following month.[53] Although inter-cameral co-ordination was limited, such appearances in the lower House, as for his spokesman Edmund Burke's great speech on conciliation with America in 1775, visibly endorsed his leadership over his supporters there.[54]

---

[44] *Proceedings and Debates*, ed. Simmons and Thomas, II, 491–4, 497–9.
[45] *Ibid.*, II, 504–6.
[46] Cobbett, XVI, 347–51.
[47] Horace Walpole, *Memoirs of the Reign of King George III*, ed. Derek Jarrett (4 vols, New Haven, 2000), III, 146.
[48] See Jeremy Black, *Pitt the Elder* (Cambridge, 1992), pp. 278–87.
[49] See John Brewer, *Party Ideology and Popular Politics at the Accession of George III* (Cambridge, 1976), pp. 77–95.
[50] O'Gorman, *Rise of Party*, pp. 222–7.
[51] Nottingham U.L., Portland papers, PwF 9016: Rockingham to Portland, 6 Mar. 1769.
[52] *L.J.*, XXXIII, 487, 669–70; Cobbett, XVII, 904–5.
[53] *L.J.*, XXXIII, 12, 23–24; *C.J.*, XXXIII, 23, 58; Cobbett, XVI, 1323.
[54] *Burke Correspondence*, III, 139: Rockingham to Burke, [22 Mar. 1775].

The 1770s witnessed a number of non-party issues in which Rockingham played a conspicuous part. Ironically, given that the matter never came before the Westminster parliament, the occasion when he exerted himself to the fullest was in the successful lobbying which he orchestrated against the imposition of a tax on Irish absentee landlords.[55] This affair smacked of obvious self-interest, but his conduct on religious issues was determined by slightly more altruistic considerations. Not only did he vote for the Dissenters' Relief Bills on 19 May 1772 (by proxy) and 2 April 1773 (in person), so establishing his broadly sympathetic views on the subscription issue,[56] but he chaired and reported from the committee on his friend Sir George Savile's Catholic Relief Bill on 27 and 28 May 1778,[57] a rare example of Rockingham being able to wrest control of a committee out of the hands of the recognized chairman and his small group of ministerialist assistants.[58] However, on the outbreak of hostilities in America, the state of parties solidified, and providing the government (as opponents) and the public (as spectators) with a respectable minority performance, hopefully boosted by a few proxy votes, became an object in itself, as an indicator of virtuous opposition. From the start of the session in late 1774, Rockingham presided over a party which nearly every year moved, and divided upon, almost the same amendment to the address in both Houses.[59]

3

Regularly opposing the address revealed a general strategic trend, under Rockingham's direction, of providing a clear presentation of ideological coherence, an aspiration which was particularly important in an era when the Rockinghamite opposition was so unpopular. The beginning can perhaps be dated to January 1770 when Rockingham, building on the momentum of the petitioning movement and imbued with the spirit of the internal party discussions which would shortly be crystallized in the publication of Burke's *Thoughts on the Cause of the Present Discontents*, overtly related the, as he saw it, diseased condition of the country to the policies pursued on the advice of the secret counsellors of the king.[60] Having with difficulty secured a day on which to summon the Lords, a procedure which was standard practice,[61] he successfully moved for a committee on the state of the nation on 22 January, speaking of the 'principle of

---

[55] Samuel J. Fanning, 'The King's Purse and the Absentee's Pocket in Eighteenth-Century Ireland', in *Crisis in the 'Great Republic'. Essays Presented to Ross J. S. Hoffman*, ed. Gaetano L. Vincitorio (New York, 1969), pp. 47–84.

[56] G. M. Ditchfield, 'The Subscription Issue in British Parliamentary Politics, 1772–79', *Parliamentary History*, VII (1988), 45–80 (esp. 56).

[57] H.L.R.O., Manuscript Minute Book, no. 125, 27 May 1778; *L.J.*, XXXV, 506, 510.

[58] John C. Sainty, *The Origin of the Office of Chairman of Committees in the House of Lords* (H.L.R.O. Memorandum no. 52, 1974).

[59] For the 1774–5 and 1775–6 sessions, see *L.J.*, XXXIV, 270, 490; *C.J.*, XXXV, 9, 399.

[60] See John Brewer, 'Party and the Double Cabinet: Two Facets of Burke's *Thoughts*', *Historical Journal*, XIV (1971), 479–501; and Frank O'Gorman, 'The Myth of Lord Bute's Secret Influence' in *Lord Bute. Essays in Re-interpretation*, ed. Karl W. Schweizer (Leicester, 1988), pp. 57–81.

[61] *L.J.*, XXXII, 403, 407. See also Rees, 'Practice and Procedure of the House of Lords', pp. 256–60.

prerogative' which lay behind all the key events of the 1760s.[62] Lord North's newly installed ministry saw off the attack in the committee on 2 February, but, as with Rockingham's (reluctant) acquiescence in Chatham's desire to address the king for a dissolution,[63] the episode signalled that he was prepared to raise the stakes both in parliament and beyond it. In the 1777–8 session, Rockingham urged in private and forwarded in the chamber itself, again with the initial support of the Chathamites, another inquiry into the state of the nation, a technique which aroused public interest. It was first debated on 2 February and after there had been numerous failed attempts to propose damaging factual resolutions, in order to publicize opposition's views, it reached a climax with Richmond's long censure motion on 7 April 1778 (the day on which Chatham dramatically collapsed).[64] In a similar way, Rockingham's synoptic speech on 19 December 1781 provided another all-encompassing survey of the nation's ills.[65]

As the 1770s continued, and parliamentary opposition came to bear the slur of disloyalty in the context of the American War of Independence, Rockingham turned increasingly to an alternative strategy of moving for inquiry into specific, rather than general, matters. It was almost impossible to oppose the war outright, but the management and conduct of it were issues ready for exploitation and, for example, Sandwich, the first lord of the admiralty, was made 'the game of opposition' in April 1779.[66] As when Rockingham moved on 16 February that year the address of thanks to Admiral Keppel, whose defence at his court martial had been championed as a party affair,[67] or in Richmond's long-running Greenwich Hospital inquiry that session,[68] the object was not merely to unveil incompetence or peculation. The argument implicit in all such causes was that public life was so riddled with corruption that the whole fabric of society was under threat. It was for this reason, too, that the civil list was taken up, as in Rockingham's detailed attack on 16 April 1777 and in the high opposition attendance and effective debating on 7 December 1779. For the idea of reducing unscrutinized royal expenditure, like the call for fewer places and pensions, was designed as an 'economical' reform which would safeguard the constitution.[69]

In hoping to vindicate his party's stance, Rockingham also sought corroborative public approval, but after the 1760s (just as in the way that the concept of a club was allowed to lapse) there was little direct use of newspapers.[70] He did give his assent to the presentation of his friends' arguments in pamphlet form, but he remained wary of the uncontrollable consequences of extended public debate, notably over the

[62] For this, Rockingham's first major recorded speech, see Cobbett, XVI, 741–5.

[63] *Correspondence of William Pitt, Earl of Chatham*, ed. William Stanhope Taylor and John Henry Pringle (4 vols, 1838–9), III, 455–7: Rockingham to Chatham, 11 and 12 May 1770.

[64] *Ibid.*, IV, 457–61: Rockingham to Chatham, 27 Nov. 1777; H.L.R.O., Manuscript Minute Book, no. 125, 2, 6, 9, 11, 16, 19 Feb.; 2, 12, 23 Mar. 1778; *L.J.*, XXXV, 287, 303, 310–12, 316–19, 333, 365–7, 388, 423–5, 428; Cobbett, XIX, 650–72, 708–18, 735–58, 818–34, 902–8, 958–69, 1012–59.

[65] Cobbett, XXII, 865–9.

[66] B.L., Add. MS 35391, ff. 17–18: Bishop Yorke of St David's to Philip Yorke, 19 Apr. 1779.

[67] *L.J.*, XXXV, 576; Cobbett, XX, 133–5.

[68] See Cobbett, XX, 508–59.

[69] *Ibid.*, XIX, 165–8; XX, 1255–66; W.W.M, R1–1869: Rockingham to Stephen Croft, 12 Dec. 1779.

[70] Brewer, *Party Ideology and Popular Politics*, pp. 227–9; Watson, 'Rise of the Opposition at Wildman's Club', p. 76.

burgeoning movement for parliamentary reform in the late 1770s.[71] Yet he joined his colleagues in defending the publication of debates in 1770 and gave some support to the re-admission of strangers to the Lords in 1774, which in itself helped to raise his profile out-of-doors.[72] Furthermore, he brought to the fore the established procedure of entering reasoned and signed protests in the minutes, which could be (and were) copied in the press. This was a device which escaped the reporting restrictions imposed on debates, provided an indirect means of exploiting the print media and avoided the expense of making direct subsidies to an opposition paper.[73] However, it also required a high degree of preparation and organization since a suitable occasion had to be chosen, the intended protest had to be drafted and entered, and the minority lords had to be cajoled into signing it at the right time.[74] No doubt the repetitive protests, mostly on America, showed up the weakness of opposition, but the long sequence entered from 1770 onwards (an average of two and a half a year) demonstrated a substantial attempt to appeal beyond parliament.[75] As Rockingham put it when complaining that he had been unable to enter one at the start of the 1775–6 session, 'the Speech and Address [which were always printed] should not pass in the Publick without our sending a Protest by way of Antedote [sic]'.[76] The revival of protesting was not as original nor as extensive as the campaign in the early 1720s,[77] but Rockingham could derive the twin satisfactions that he was keeping a small band of followers publicly committed to his party and had regularly put on record their rearguard efforts.[78]

Another possible strategy was a party 'secession', ideally conceived of as a dignified abstention from Parliament in order to make a clear and public disavowal of the whole conduct of the executive. Writing to William Dowdeswell, the party leader in the Commons, on 30 October 1772, Rockingham optimistically argued that a secession would 'much alarm the ministry – would force Several Parts of Opposition into more attention towards us, & would also apprize the Publick of the danger they are in'.[79] At the nadir of his fortunes in mid-1775, he was reluctant to attend parliament until

---

[71] Brewer, *Party Ideology and Popular Politics*, pp. 229–33, 237–8; Hannah Barker, *Newspapers, Politics, and Public Opinion in Late Eighteenth-Century England* (Oxford, 1998), p. 135.

[72] William C. Lowe, 'Peers and Printers: The Beginnings of Sustained Press Coverage of the House of Lords in the 1770s', *Parliamentary History*, VII (1988), 241–56.

[73] William C. Lowe, 'The House of Lords, Party, and Public Opinion: Opposition Use of the Protest, 1760–1782', *Albion*, XI (1979), 143–56.

[74] For examples of these three elements in the process, see W.W.M., R1–1482: Dowdeswell to Rockingham, 8 Apr. 1774 (printed in George Thomas [Keppel], Earl of Albemarle, *Memoirs of the Marquis of Rockingham and his Contemporaries* (2 vols, 1852) [hereafter *Rockingham Memoirs*], II, 240–1); R1–1559: Richmond to Rockingham, 12 Mar. 1775; R1–1490: Richmond to Rockingham, [18 May 1774].

[75] Counting 33 entirely or partially Rockinghamite protests, out of 53 altogether, over 13 sessions (1770–82): Ditchfield, 'Lords in the Age of the American Revolution', pp. 201, 230–3; *A Complete Collection of the Protests of the House of Lords*, ed. James E. Thorold Rogers (3 vols, Oxford, 1875), II, 99–213.

[76] W.W.M., R1–1615: Rockingham to Camden, [27 Oct. 1775] (quoted in Lowe, 'House of Lords, Party, and Public Opinion', p. 50).

[77] *Peers, Politics and Power*, ed. Jones and Jones, p. 231; Ditchfield, 'Lords in the Age of the American Revolution', p. 231.

[78] The names of the 20 most frequent signatories are listed in Elofson, *Rockingham Connection*, p. 198.

[79] W.W.M., R1–1409.

the people should have seen through their deluded approval of the war, but later that autumn he recommended that a token dissent be made from the address and advocated that 'a joynt Memorial, or Remonstrance, or Petition should be drawn up & sign'd by Members of Parlt. of both Houses, & presented to his Majesty'.[80] That the secession of 1776–7 and similar steps failed was largely due to the popularity of the government and the disunity of opposition, but an essential part of Rockingham's general strategy was that parliamentary activities should be given a wider airing; so that, for instance, if a certain address were defeated in parliament, he recommended that 'it should be laid before the Publick immediately afterwards'.[81] On more than one occasion, he and his party were publicly thanked for their sustained campaigns at Westminster, suggesting that they did have an impact in the outside community.[82]

4

From the late 1770s there was a gradual deterioration of the ministerial solidity in both Houses, which made it imperative for the Rockingham whigs to assert their own identity within the opposition. Even before that time, they had evolved certain forms of organization in the Lords, and although the evidence is sketchy, these were mostly overseen by their titular head, partly because there were few other active peers in the party. It would have been he who hosted the discussions or co-ordinated the correspondence which preceded parliamentary activities, following no doubt on Newcastle's example in the 1760s.[83] Frequent meetings were held on a more or less formal basis, to which leading party members were summoned, in order to make important tactical decisions,[84] and, when time pressed, consultations were sometimes left to the last minute in the chamber.[85] Deputizing for the absent Rockingham at various times in the early 1770s, Richmond eagerly undertook a number of duties, holding party dinners and the like, which were probably regular features of opposition organization.[86] Most interestingly of all, at a time when summoning friends was more usually done by written or personal contact,[87] was Richmond's apparently off-hand reference to an opposition 'whip' in a letter to Rockingham on 3 May 1771 about

---

[80] *Ibid.*, R1–1569: Rockingham to Manchester, 28 June; R1–1600: Rockingham to Burke, 11 Sept.; R1–1601: Rockingham to Lord John Cavendish, 18 Sept. 1775.

[81] *Ibid.*, R1–1976: Rockingham to unknown (undated draft).

[82] E.g., by the City of London: see Alison Gilbert Olson, *The Radical Duke. Career and Correspondence of Charles Lennox, Third Duke of Richmond* (Oxford, 1961), pp. 176–7: Richmond to Shelburne, 16 Jan. 1780.

[83] W.W.M., R1–782, 789: Newcastle to Rockingham, 4, [29] May 1767.

[84] Ditchfield, 'Lords in the Age of the American Revolution', pp. 228–9. For e.g.s of summons, see H.M.C., *14th Report, Appendix, Part X*, pp. 70, 554–5: Rockingham to Dartmouth, 4 [and 5] Feb. 1770, 13 May 1767.

[85] E.g., W.W.M., R1–1820 (printed in *Rockingham Memoirs*, II, 377–9): Rockingham to Manchester, 29 Mar. 1779.

[86] E.g., W.W.M., R1–1358: Richmond to Rockingham, 12 Feb.; R1–1361: Burke to Rockingham, [16 Feb.] 1771.

[87] There were many occasions on which lords were summoned to attend on particular debates; e.g., R1–791: Newcastle to Rockingham, [23 May 1767]; H.M.C., *14th Report, Appendix, Part X*, p. 64: Rockingham to Dartmouth, 12 Dec. 1768; Nottingham U.L., Portland papers, PwF 9118: Rockingham to Portland, 7 Dec. 1777.

the New Shoreham Bill. He wrote that, 'As I know Your mind is so much taken up ... I thought of sending cards myself (one of which I inclose), but wish to have Your advise [sic]', implying that the use of party 'cards' was standard procedure and that it was Rockingham who issued them.[88] For much of the time, however, Rockingham was less of a driving force than a visible focus, as can be illustrated by the fact that in the House itself, where there was a relaxed attitude to the formal seating requirements, it was natural for his supporters to congregate together in a group around him.[89]

Such overt signs of party coherence became especially vital in a House which was increasingly hostile to ministers. This sometimes necessitated the foregoing of co-operation with other parties, as when Rockingham, in annoyance at the lack of prior consultation in early 1775, informed Chatham that he would promise no more than his personal attendance on the latter's bill to settle the troubles in America.[90] By accepting the reality of independence, Rockingham created an ideological gulf with him, and although he sometimes still acted in alliance with Lord Shelburne, Chatham's successor, personal differences and rivalries made such relations problematic.[91] The extension of the war to France and Spain was the principal reason for the precipitation into opposition of various former ministers, ex-Bedfordites and independents, and Rockingham tried to take at least some of them under his wing.[92] The groundswell of participation from these former government supporters meant that he had to be more active in order to keep ahead of the field,[93] and this, plus the generally larger attendances of lords, was perhaps what lay behind the higher number of divisions (in 1777–8 and 1778–9), for many of which the Rockinghams had a specific teller, Lord Effingham.[94] In attempting to mark out a specific identity for himself and his party, it was significant that Rockingham insisted on certain pre-conditions for entering office during the abortive negotiations in 1780.[95]

Rockingham also had to assert his personal authority, as despite his ability to get his own way in party consultations,[96] he was sometimes implicitly criticized for inertia by his more active supporters, such as Charles James Fox.[97] But, among his friends, he gained many plaudits, and his character and the intangible effect of his presence and hard work in the chamber, as (before he fell ill) over the Royal Marriages Bill in

[88] W.W.M., R1–1375, with the 'card' at R1–1376.

[89] Rees, 'Practice and Procedure of the House of Lords', pp. 302–5. On this subject, see Clyve Jones, 'Seating Problems in the House of Lords in the Early Eighteenth Century: The Evidence of the Manuscript Minutes', *B.I.H.R.*, LI (1978), 132–45.

[90] W.W.M., R1–1544 (printed in *Rockingham Memoirs*, II, 270): Rockingham to Chatham, [31 Jan. 1775].

[91] See John Norris, *Shelburne and Reform* (New York, 1963), pp. 95–8, 132–5.

[92] E.g., W.W.M., R1–1945: Rockingham to Temple, 16 Jan. 1781.

[93] *Ibid.*, R1–1976: Rockingham to unknown (undated draft).

[94] Ditchfield, 'Lords in the Age of the American Revolution', pp. 226, 230; John C. Sainty and David Dewar, *Divisions in the House of Lords* (H.L.R.O. Occasional Publications no. 2, 1976).

[95] See Ian R. Christie, 'The Marquis of Rockingham and Lord North's Offer of a Coalition, June–July 1780', *E.H.R.*, LXIX (1954), 388–407.

[96] W.W.M., R1–1540 (printed in *Rockingham Memoirs*, II, 268–9): Richmond to Rockingham, 28 Jan. 1775.

[97] W.W.M., R1–1686 (printed in *Rockingham Memoirs*, II, 297–8): Fox to Rockingham, 13 Oct. 1776.

1772,⁹⁸ must have had a strong motivating effect on his followers.⁹⁹ He was, in any case, the recognized head of the party, being contacted as such over parliamentary proceedings by the government leader, Lord Rochford.¹⁰⁰ In addition, many of his high profile actions in the Lords, as when he himself moved the amendment to the address in 1775, 1776 and 1779, emphasized his leading position.¹⁰¹ He was not afraid to take on ministers; for instance, standing his ground when he rose at the same time as the colonial secretary Lord Dartmouth, on 7 February 1775, to try to present American merchants' petitions (and protesting at his being defeated on the previous question).¹⁰² On 16 February 1778, in an example of how opposition attempted to surprise ministers, he read to the Lords the American General Horatio Gates's letter calling for independence to be granted.¹⁰³ Condemning the peace commissioners' manifesto on 7 December, he struck an unusually personal note by declaring that the threat to desolate the colonies was contrary to the teachings of Christ.¹⁰⁴ The following year, having raised the matter directly with the king, he brought up the issue of Irish distress in a motion on 11 May, when he agreed to a compromise amendment in order to secure its unanimous approval.¹⁰⁵ He made plain his pretensions to be seen as a 'principal' in negotiations for office, and Shelburne was always made to understand that Rockingham was destined for the treasury in any future administration.¹⁰⁶

In a party with very few effective speakers, apart from Richmond, Rockingham's contributions in debate were vital to how the party positioned itself, especially against Shelburne. But the nature and timing of his speeches, a perhaps neglected aspect of parliamentary management, also had an internal party dimension. His friends encouraged him to become a regular speaker, not least because of the conviction which he was capable of instilling in his audience,¹⁰⁷ and, despite his reputation for lassitude, Rockingham could exert himself by making preparations and did speak in almost all the major debates from the mid-1770s.¹⁰⁸ For instance, on the technical question of the Annuity and Lottery Bill, he borrowed papers from John Hewett, former M.P. for Nottinghamshire, telling him on 20 March 1781 that 'I must lock myself up tonight, as I mean to say a few words on the Subject in the H. of Lords tomorrow':¹⁰⁹ on the 21st, presumably from the notes he had written beforehand,

⁹⁸ Hoffman, *The Marquis*, pp. 274–7.
⁹⁹ *Burke Correspondence*, III, 108: Burke to Rockingham, [24 Jan. 1775].
¹⁰⁰ W.W.M., R1–1619: Rochford to Rockingham, 30 Oct. 1775.
¹⁰¹ Cobbett, XVIII, 708, 1369–70; XX, 1027–33.
¹⁰² *L.J.*, XXXIV, 305–8; Cobbett, XVIII, 265–94.
¹⁰³ *L.J.*, XXXV, 310; Cobbett, XIX, 730–3.
¹⁰⁴ Cobbett, XX, 1–9.
¹⁰⁵ *L.J.*, XXXV, 732; Cobbett, XX, 635–42; W.W.M., R1–1830(a): Rockingham to William Denham, 26 May 1779.
¹⁰⁶ Norris, *Shelburne and Reform*, pp. 114, 152.
¹⁰⁷ W.W.M., R1–1169 (printed in *Rockingham Memoirs*, II, 91–2): Richmond to Rockingham, 10 Mar. 1769.
¹⁰⁸ 'Draft' speeches, mostly factual notes and lists of headings (or prompts), are gathered together at W.W.M., R81.
¹⁰⁹ *Ibid.*, R1–1958 and Nottinghamshire Archives, Foljambe papers, DD.FJ 11/1/1 pt. 1, ff. 75, 77, 78: Rockingham to Hewett, 17, 18, 20 Mar. 1781.

he made a substantial statistical statement against the loan.[110] In fact, in at least half of the debates Rockingham left it to Richmond or others to reply (or to initiate opposition resolutions), and instead spoke late in the sitting. This approach allowed him to correct the wrong impression given by, for instance, the wayward duke of Manchester or the maverick independent, Lord Abingdon.[111] As the party's speakers tended to be on the 'liberal' side, it was crucial for Rockingham to restate his moderate position as to their policies,[112] and this was especially true in relation to the more extreme and excitable Richmond.[113] For example, although he gave no overt reaction to Richmond's Reform Bill on 2 June 1780, the next day he rebuffed the former's suggestion, in the discussion on the Gordon Riots, in favour of the immediate repeal of the Quebec Act.[114] Again, in the debate on Germain's peerage on 18 February 1782, Rockingham's intervention may have been confused, but it did effectively deflate Richmond's injudicious enthusiasm on this divisive matter.[115] Apart from setting straight his party's ideological position, particularly for those outside the chamber, Rockingham's speeches also served to encapsulate a recognizably 'Rockinghamite' mentality.

5

The final capitulation of the North ministry in the dying stages of the American war should have been the signal for the triumphant return of Rockingham to power as the undisputed head of a coherent ministry. That this did not occur was partly because Rockingham was already very ill, and so, for instance, was unable to undertake detailed preparations for managing the upper chamber,[116] where, indeed, he was not often present and rarely spoke.[117] The other major factor was the dominance of Shelburne, who as home secretary became the *de facto* 'leader' in the Lords,[118] and at least once had to present royal messages in Rockingham's absence.[119] The administration did achieve notable results, fulfilling its previously stated intentions by beginning the peace negotiations, passing several measures of 'economical' reform and granting legislative independence to Ireland. Yet George III's intimacy with Shelburne weakened the Rockinghamite element in what was in fact an unbalanced coalition; one indicator of the lack of royal confidence was that only a single close supporter

[110] W.W.M., R81-14, 15, 18, 19, 21–9 (notes), 20 (headings), 13, 30 (draft or corrected version); Cobbett, XXI, 1379–86.

[111] Notably in the 1779–80 session, when he spoke late in seven out of ten major debates.

[112] E.g. on 18 May 1770: see Richmond and Rockingham's speeches in Cobbett, XVI, 1010–12, 1020–2.

[113] See Olson, *Radical Duke*, esp. pp. 9, 12–13, 29–32, 37–47, 59–60, 64–6, 90.

[114] Cobbett, XXI, 664–9, 684.

[115] See *Burke Correspondence*, IV, 404–5: Burke to Rockingham, [18 Feb. 1782].

[116] There were about 40 peers, out of the 351 present, at his first levée, 11 Apr. 1782, which he may have considered as the equivalent of a 'pre-sessional' meeting: W.W.M., R1–2043.

[117] He was listed as present on only 18 (or 28 per cent) of the 65 days on which the Lords sat during his premiership (11 Apr.-28 June 1782): *L.J.*, XXXVI, 428–551.

[118] Sainty, 'Origin of the Leadership', pp. 61, 71.

[119] On 2 May 1782: *L.J.*, XXXVI, 454.

of the prime minister (Admiral Keppel) was given a peerage.[120] Rockingham's death on 1 July and the ignominious break up of the government have contributed to his poor reputation, but given his state of health and the ministerial instability of the two subsequent years, his record in his second term of office should not be allowed to overshadow his previous career.[121]

Rather, as has been done in this article, it is important to relate Rockingham's role as a party leader in the Lords to the problems of parliamentary opposition in the 1760s and 1770s. This was a period during which the struggle for office was expected to be largely fruitless and, as Grayson Ditchfield has correctly observed, the aim was the 'preservation of identity and the prevention of desertions', at a time when 'survival as much as recruitment was the objective'.[122] By any standards, Rockingham's handling of the practices of opposition was weak. On technical matters, having been an inadequate 'leader' of the Lords, he rarely made sufficient pre-sessional preparations for opposition nor properly exploited lists and surveys, although he was adequate in his management of proxies. Organizationally, too, he failed to win control of the 'party of the crown' when in office and only intermittently co-ordinated his party's activities between the two Houses or managed directly its activities in the Lords itself, despite being generally successful in carving out a distinct niche for the Rockinghams. However, the practices of opposition, which were often of limited value, were usually made subordinate to the wider purposes of opposition, on which Rockingham's record was undoubtedly much better. Thus, in terms of parliamentary debates, although he made little sustained use of the Lords on cross-party issues, he occasionally allied himself effectively with other opposition groups and did make an impact in employing motions for both general and specific inquiries. Finally, when it came to the issue of appealing beyond parliament, the various secessions may have come to nothing, but the employment of protests and, in particular, Rockingham's high profile leadership and his espousal of moderate lines of policy, can be classed as successful. The practices and purposes of leadership cannot always be clearly separated from each other,[123] but he certainly did better in the second of these respects in the later part of his career, undoubtedly because of the 'conscientious satisfaction' that he took in continuing to act and to hope for better days.[124] And if his attention to practical opposition was sporadic – politics was, in any case, not a continuous activity – his ideological commitment was sincerely held and consistently applied for party purposes.

---

[120] Although four other peerages were granted in Apr. and June 1782: J. C. Sainty, *Peerage Creations, 1649–1800. A Chronological List of Creations in the Peerages of England and Great Britain* (Parliamentary History Occasional Publications no. 1, 1998), pp. 68–9. On the relationship between royal confidence and new peerages, see William C. Lowe, 'George III, Peerage Creations and Politics, 1760–1784', *Historical Jour.*, XXXV (1992), 587–609.

[121] O'Gorman, *Rise of Party*, pp. 463–4.

[122] Ditchfield, 'Lords in the Age of the American Revolution', p. 228. See Pares, *King George III and the Politicians*, pp. 60, 83–4.

[123] E.g., see W.W.M., R1–1486 and 1487 (printed in *Rockingham Memoirs*, II, 242–5): Manchester to Rockingham and draft reply, 20 Apr. 1774.

[124] The phrase occurs (in relation to the American war) in W.W.M., R1–1610: Rockingham to [? John Scudamore], 16 Oct. 1775.

Rockingham's leadership of a viable opposition was not unprecedented and, for instance, it displayed many features of the active management and 'country' ideology of Earl Cowper's intensive (indeed, more intensive, but non-party) role in the early 1720s.[125] However, Rockingham was the first long-term party leader in opposition, heading a persistent, sometimes dangerous, challenge to ministers for 16 years. Of course, that he led the party for so long was not necessarily an achievement to be proud of, since the point of opposition was always ultimately to overthrow the existing administration. Yet there was almost no one else of sufficient calibre or standing to have done the job, and it is possible that the connexion would have been re-submerged into some form of court whig administration by the only realistic alternatives, and far more active and capable politicians, Newcastle (had he not been side-lined before his death in 1768) or Richmond (who did this in the early 1780s).[126] In addition, if Rockingham contributed to the armoury of opposition techniques and to the tradition of dignified resistance, his immediate successors as party leaders in the Lords were disappointing in their lack of application and purpose (albeit in even more adverse circumstances).[127] So much depended upon personal factors, and it was mainly Rockingham's charm and forbearance, his 'mild captaincy',[128] that enabled him to claim the headship of this alliance of disparate personalities over a prolonged period. As Richmond remarked to Burke on 15 November 1772, 'I believe our greatest Bond is the Pride of the individuals, which Unfortunately tho' it keeps us from breaking, hinders us from acting like men of Sense. The marquis manages us better than any Man can, but he will never make us what we ought to be, the Thing is not practicable.'[129]

---

[125] Clyve Jones, 'The New Opposition in the House of Lords, 1720–3', *Historical Jour.*, XXXVI (1993), 309–29, and *idem*, 'William, First Earl Cowper, Country Whiggery, and the Leadership of the Opposition in the House of Lords, 1720–1723', in *Lords of Parliament. Studies, 1714–1914*, ed. Richard W. Davis (Stamford, 1995), pp. 29–43.

[126] Langford, *First Rockingham Administration*, pp. 279–80; Olson, *Radical Duke*, pp. 66–72.

[127] Michael W. McCahill, *Order and Equipoise. The Peerage and the House of Lords, 1783–1806* (1978), pp. 7–8, 119–28.

[128] J. Steven Watson, *The Reign of George III, 1760–1815* (Oxford, 1960), p. 113.

[129] *Burke Correspondence*, II, 371.

William, First Lord Grenville

MICHAEL W. McCAHILL

In 1974 Sir John Sainty delineated the functions of the office of leader of the house of lords and acknowledged the special contribution of William, first Lord Grenville in establishing that post as distinct and important.[1] From the late seventeenth century, one peer – usually the northern secretary – assumed responsibility for maintaining lists of members, finding peers to move and second addresses, arranging for attendance and the distribution of proxies, preparing reports for the king on the Lords' proceedings and keeping important supporters informed on government policies. According to Sainty, Grenville elevated the post to a new level: in addition to performing the traditional chores, he served for the first time as the government's principal spokesman in the House on all important matters.

In fact, Grenville's role as leader extended beyond the duties Sainty identified. He contributed to the effective conduct of business there by maintaining control over the Lords' calendar and agenda, by reviewing controversial legislation and, where necessary, forcing amendments on sponsors and, finally, by working closely with the several speakers of the Commons to maintain harmony between the two houses. In addition, he devised a representative peerage system for the Irish free from some at least of the anomalies that plagued the Scottish peerage. In office and in opposition, Grenville enjoyed a special, authoritative status on account of his mastery of the whole range of important issues, the time and energy he devoted to the House and because of his persuasive speaking abilities. He used that status not only to uphold the ministerial position but later to create a nucleus of support for some of the important but controversial issues that divided the Lords during the first three or four decades of the nineteenth century. A firm defender of the House and of the special role and position of the peerage, Grenville nevertheless became more aware of the legitimacy of public opinion: not only did he exploit that opinion where it reinforced the positions he favored; over time, he induced the House, at least tentatively, to acknowledge it as an influence that could and should affect their own deliberations. Among the 17 peers who led the house of lords during the reign of George III at least three leaders – Newcastle, Rockingham and the second earl of Liverpool – surpassed Grenville in political stature. None, however, had the same profound, transforming impact on the House itself, and none did more to assist the House in the transition from one political world into another.

It was Pitt rather than Grenville who first saw the need to enlarge the compass of the leader's role in the house of lords. His first two leaders there, Viscount Sydney

---

[1] J. C. Sainty, 'The Origins of the Leadership of the House of Lords, *Bulletin of the Institute of Historical Research*, XLVII (1974), 53–73.

and the duke of Leeds, performed the traditional role of leader adequately but lacked political stature and were weak, reluctant debaters. Real authority in the Lords rested with the formidable but increasingly wayward Chancellor Thurlow who dominated its debates and legislative deliberations. Unfortunately, by 1788 these three along with Lord Hawkesbury were disenchanted with Pitt's leadership, his espousal of slave trade abolition and his failure to consult them sufficiently. Thurlow flirted briefly with the whigs during the regency crisis and in 1789 complained of the slovenly manner in which the Tobacco Bill and other revenue measures were drafted.[2] Not surprisingly in these circumstances, Pitt pressed the king on the need 'to remedy the inconveniences which have for some time been felt from the want of a regular conduct of the detail of business in the House of Lords'. The solution, he continued lay in the placement of a suitable person there 'to attend constantly to the conduct of of [sic] all domestick business' who would also mollify Thurlow. Grenville's 'temper and discretion', he concluded, qualified him for both tasks. The combination of an expanded role for the leader and Grenville's presence in the Lords soon led, as Pitt had hoped, to a ministerial presence that possessed 'more strength than has belonged to us since the beginning of the Government'.[3]

Grenville brought many assets to his new position. Unlike Sydney or Leeds, he was a central figure in the government; by 1790 he stood second to Pitt himself and throughout the next decade he formed with Pitt and Dundas the government's inner circle. He was, as his biographer says, 'formidably well informed', in part because of experience gained over a decade as chief secretary in Ireland, paymaster general, vice-president of the board of trade, speaker of the house of commons and home secretary, in part because of his own serious study. His role in the formulation of policy extended far beyond his departmental responsibilities; thus, he was able as no leader was before him to speak authoritatively on the whole range of issues that came before parliament. Diligent and energetic, he presented a happy contrast to the lackadaisical Leeds. As a member of a powerful if controversial family and an increasingly effective leader in the House, he possessed a base that enabled him over time to maintain at least a measure of independence from Pitt.[4] Finally, despite his reputed cold aloofness, Grenville was a zealous, even passionate advocate of ideas to which he was committed, ranging from a need for strong continental allies in the war against France during the 1790s to catholic emancipation, slave trade abolition and free trade in the early decades of the nineteenth century. While his opinions, especially on the latter reforms, alienated many in the house, they drew to him a band of personal adherents as well as an array of more loosely connected allies.

---

[2] *Lords of Parliament. Studies, 1714–1914*, ed. R. W. Davis (Stanford, 1995), pp. 72–6; John Ehrman, *The Younger Pitt: I. The Years of Acclaim* (New York, 1969), pp. 621–2; Peter Jupp, *Lord Grenville 1759–1934* (Oxford, 1985), pp. 98–100; M. W. McCahill, *Order and Equipoise. The Peerage and the House of Lords, 1783–1806* (1978), pp. 115–6, 130–8.

[3] *The Later Correspondence of George III*, ed. A. Aspinall (5 vols, Cambridge, 1962–70) I, 501–2; Earl Stanhope, *The Life of the Rt. Hon. William Pitt* (3 vols, 1879), I, 337–8.

[4] Ehrman, *Pitt*, I, 122–3, 310–1; idem, *The Younger Pitt: II – The Reluctant Transition* (Stanford, 1983), pp. 530–5; idem, *The Younger Pitt: III – The Consuming Struggle* (Stanford, 1996), p. 36; Jupp, *Grenville*, pp. 97–8, 102, 187, 414–5, 452; McCahill, *Order and Equipoise*, pp. 135–8.

Along with these strengths, Grenville had his share of weaknesses. He suffered on account of his family's unpopularity, its notorious appetite for honours and largesse and its arrogance. George III lamented that Grenvilles 'must govern despotically, or oppose Government violently', a tendency he attributed to their greed and extreme obstinacy – qualities he claimed Lord Grenville possessed in abundance. Nor was the king unique in his judgments: Malmesbury complained of Grenville's lack of empathy, the first earl of Liverpool of his coldness, his offensive manner and his rapaciousness and Lord Hutchinson dismissed him as a 'dull, stupid fellow'.[5] Grenville himself acknowledged his shortcomings as a politician in 1807: 'I want one great and essential quality for my station, and every hour increases the difficulty. I can still, and could still, for a few years, as long as my eyesight is spared to me, labour at my desk, but I am not competent to the management of men. I never was so naturally, and toil and anxiety more and more unfit me for it.' Like Pitt, Grenville had a cold public manner; however, Canning noted at their first meeting that this frosty demeanor arose more from shyness than pride. In private Grenville was a warm, thoughtful associate; unfortunately, many did not find their way into his inner circle. His second shortcoming as a political leader derived from his ambivalence about politics and the pursuit of power. By the mid-1790s he had attained high office and achieved financial security as a result of marriage and a rich sinecure. Thereafter, Grenville's political appetite diminished: Lord Chancellor Loughborough attributed his resignation in 1801 at least partially to his addiction 'to study', and William Eden later noted with astonishment Grenville's enthusiasm for gardening and the country. Thus, it is not surprising that within 12 months of the talents' installation, he was sick of office or that his frequent absences from the House later caused complaints among his whig allies there.[6]

Given these deficiencies, Grenville's careful attention to the needs and attendance of his followers in the House was all the more surprising. On his appointment, the routine business of summoning peers passed into the hands of a succession of clerks, first in the home and subsequently in the foreign office.[7] However, unlike his successors later in the nineteenth century, Grenville served as chief whip in the Lords as well as its leader: the efforts of a succession of clerks did not relieve him of the burden of securing attendances for important contests, especially when those took place at the beginning and end of the session. Certain peers did not heed the official summons but expected to receive personal appeals from the leader. Though

---

[5] *The Diaries of Sylvester Douglas (Lord Glenbervie)*, ed. F. Bickley (2 vols, 1928), I, 149–50, 176; *The Journal and Correspondence of William, Lord Auckland*, ed. the bishop of Bath and Wells (4 vols, 1862), IV, 308; *Diaries and correspondence of James Harris, 1st Earl of Malmesbury*, ed. 3rd earl of Malmesbury (4 vols, 1844), IV, 324. Public Record Office of Northern Ireland, Donoughmore Papers, T/3459/F/13/37. A number of historians have made similar conclusions about Grenville. See, for example, Piers Mackesy, *War Without Victory. The Downfall of Pitt 1799–1802* (Oxford, 1984), pp. 22, 177–8; A. S. Turberville, *The House of Lords in the Age of Reform 1784–1837* (1958), p. 68.

[6] *Memoirs of the Courts and Cabinets of George III*, ed. the duke of Buckingham (4 vols, 1853), III, 133; *The Letter Journal of George Canning, 1793–1795*, ed. P. Jupp, (Camden 4th ser., XLI, 1991), pp. 28–9; *Glenbervie Diaries*, ed. Bickley, I, 169; *Auckland Correspondence*, ed. Bath and Wells, IV, 314–5; Jupp, *Grenville*, p. 409; B.L., Add. MS 51593, ff. 50–1, 18.

[7] Charles Brietzche and Charles Goddard, home office clerks, performed these duties in 1790–1. When Grenville moved to the foreign office T. Bidwell (1791–2), J. Hinchcliffe (1792–5) and J. W. Hay (1795–1801) summoned peers. I am grateful to Sir John Sainty for sharing this information.

government forces after 1794 outnumbered their opponents in the house of lords, sometimes by a margin of 5:1, it was important that a substantial body of peers affirm ministerial policies relating to the war and domestic security. Grenville solicited the attendance for such contests, showing in the process that he appreciated the toll of attendance on the aged, the ill or those who were occupied with other matters. Thus, he was careful to notify supporters when their presence was unnecessary. As a result of his careful attention Pitt's government sustained overwhelming majorities during the 1790s as did the ministry of the talents during its first parliamentary session. During the early months of the talents' ministry Fox worried that a strong opposition, bolstered by the court, might attract as many as 60 supporters in the Lords. In fact, under Grenville's leadership the administration carried Windham's controversial Army Bill there by a majority of 91–34.[8]

Because the House permitted absent peers to vote by proxy, Grenville, like earlier leaders, had to arrange for their collection and distribution. Rules relating to proxies were complex, even confusing, and the task was an onerous one that required constant attention. Peers wishing to vote by proxy had to submit a new form each session; personal attendance vacated existing proxies, so upon leaving London, peers had to bestow new ones. No peer could hold more than two proxies of his fellows, and an attentive leader had to solicit new proxies from the absent lords when the colleague who had held their votes was out of town. Not only did Grenville collect proxies: he explained the system to peers who misused it or did not understand the process; more importantly, he arranged for their distribution among those who attended regularly or saw to their transfers on the rare occasions when a peer placed his proxy in the wrong hands. His correspondence demonstrates that Grenville was attentive, efficient and endlessly patient in fulfilling these tasks and that his close relationship with Henry Cowper, one of the clerks, eased this burden.[9]

The leadership carried with it a number of other minor routine duties. At least occasionally he prepared reports for the king on the Lords' proceedings: perhaps because of more extensive press coverage of debates in the House these reports were intermittent; few remain among his papers or the printed correspondence of George III. He apparently hosted dinners on the night before the sessions' opening until 1799 and certainly advised associates on the line to take at debates. He also struggled with the tiresome duty of finding peers to move and second the Lords' addresses to the king, sometimes with Pitt's assistance. This task was especially difficult: government sought supporters who did not hold office to move or second its addresses, but many of these peers were reluctant to speak in the House despite the fact that Grenville provided the material on which to base their remarks and even coached them prior to their appearances. Long after he left office he continued to instruct new peers or those who recently had inherited a peerage on how to take their seats in the House.

However, Pitt sent his cousin to the Lords not merely to serve as a glorified whip but to take charge of 'conduct of public business' there. Already well versed in the

---

[8] B.L., Add. MS 59359, f. 21; Add. MS 59362, ff. 135, 139–41; Add. MS 58955, ff. 41–2; Add. MS 59364, f. 56; Add. MS 58940, f. 112; Add. MS 47569, ff. 275–8.

[9] B.L., Add. MS 59362, ff. 143–7; Add. MS 59366, ff. 145, 169; Add. MS 59369, ff. 13, 29; Add. MS 58979, ff. 52–7; Jupp, *Grenville*, pp. 129–31.

intricacies of parliamentary procedure as a result of his brief stint as the Commons' speaker, Grenville quickly established himself as the master of the Lords' procedures. As a result, he was able not only to insure the regularity of proceedings there but to thwart or silence his opponents. For example, in 1806 he rejected a motion introduced by Hawkesbury, the opposition leader, that the House solicit the opinion of generals on Windham's army reforms on the grounds that such queries were contrary to its procedures; peers could probe witnesses for information, he noted, not for opinions. In December of the same year he dismissed a motion introduced by the earl of Radnor to vote an address to the king on the death of the duke of Brunswick because his review of the *Journals* showed there was no precedent for the House condoling the monarch on the death of a foreign-born relative. Two months later, when the earl of Warwick moved for a committee to examine proposals for new systems of taxation, Grenville retorted that the House could not consider such a motion because there were no papers currently before it that members could refer to the committee as the basis for its study. While in office and in opposition, he interrupted the speeches of his opponents on the grounds that one or more of their remarks were out of order and in this way either silenced his adversaries or disrupted the flow of their remarks.[10]

As leader, Grenville had wide latitude in arranging the calendar of business in the House. Naturally, he co-ordinated the flow of business with his principal colleagues, but there was also a tradition of communication between ministers in the Lords and leading opposition peers in setting the Lords' agenda. To a degree, Grenville honoured this tradition. During the 1790s he was often flexible in his negotiations with whig leaders and apologetic when his own absence necessitated a rescheduling of debates. However, he did not hesitate either to impose his decisions or to exploit his superior knowledge of parliamentary procedure to get his way. He was prepared over the objection of opponents to set dates for consideration of their motions according to the convenience of colleagues such as the chancellor, and he did not indefinitely tolerate his opponents' delaying tactics. Impatient in May 1806 with the obstructive tactics of the anti-abolitionists in the House, he instructed his deputy, Lord Auckland, to set specific dates for the Foreign Slave Trade Bill's passage, adding that he should ignore demands of the duke of Clarence and others for further postponement. On other occasions, his manner of settling the Lords' agenda was as devious as it was deft. Thus, Lord Fitzwilliam reported with admiration as well as annoyance that:

> Ld Grenville has maneuvered with considerable dexterity: by announcing to the House that on *Monday* next he shall propose to appoint for consideration of the Resolutions, He puts the House off its guard, & gains the point of *fixing a day* for the consideration *without debate*. He does not summon the House for the question, which he is aware will be the principal question, but surreptitiously carries an

---

[10] Hansard, *Parl. Debs*, VII, 607, 1088–9; VIII, 34, 1030. In fact, Grenville occasionally dictated to both Houses on procedural matters. The Irish union required alterations to the Commons and a new locale for the Lords. However, after the Lords adopted a motion similar to the Commons' and voted to establish a committee, Grenville told Pitt that any alteration in the king's palace had to proceed from him, and that Pitt in the Commons and he in the Lords should present royal messages to the effect that the Lords would move temporarily to the Court of Requests. Only after receiving that message could each house establish its committee. B.L., Add. MS 58938, ff. 200–1.

apparent unanimity, as to the important point of taking them all into consideration. We are not so much as apprized of the day, when he will name the day for the consideration, so that if those who are adverse to any discussion, do not stand sentry at the House, without relief, that important point is gain'd as a matter of course, & it goes forth as if the House had unanimously adopted the measure as fit for discussion.[11]

If tactical considerations determined Grenville's arrangement of the Lords' calendar, he was also concerned to insure the steady and expeditious flow of the business of the House. This latter preoccupation was especially apparent while he served as first lord of the treasury. Thus, in 1806 he favored the introduction in the Lords of a bill indemnifying officials for permitting direct trade between the United States and West Indian islands as a means of saving legislative time; the Commons already had a mass of legislation under consideration. In June of the same year he gave notice that he would bring in during the following session a bill for the reform of the Scottish court of session, in part because the many judicial appeals from Scotland accumulated in London, clogging the Lords' calendar and causing great delay for suitors waiting for a resolution to their cases. The following January he impatiently instructed Auckland to bring forward as many bills as possible from the treasury, the admiralty and other departments early in the session: 'let us exhibit', he added, 'for once in this World, a short session with an efficient completion of much important business'. The government's subsequent imbroglio with the king over concessions to roman catholics thwarted the fulfillment of this objective.[12]

As Grenville established himself in the House he gained a larger measure of authority not only over the schedule of proceedings but even over the content of legislation. Opposition members appealed to him for relief from the obstruction of the various government lawyers in the House, and commoners looked to him to disentangle legislation tied up in the Lords for procedural reasons.[13] Grenville introduced amendments in pending legislation at the behest of important colleagues and reviewed with them alterations proposed by other peers. He met with members of both Houses to hear their concerns regarding pending legislation, passing their recommendations on to relevant ministers; he also negotiated with them regarding amendments they proposed to government bills. In turn, ministers and others not only submitted their legislation to him for his prior approval but usually accepted the alterations he recommended. It was understandable, perhaps, that Auckland and other ministers in the talents should submit legislation to their superior and adopt the changes he proposed. But his authority extended beyond his own immediate colleagues. After watching Chancellor Loughborough's fussy obstruction tie up his Census Bill for a week in the Lords in December 1800, Charles Abbot met with Grenville 'and settled with him the plan of amendments, and of a new Population Bill', necessitated by the Lords' alterations to the original bill's money clauses. Within

---

[11] B.L., Add. MS 59366, ff. 153–5; Add. MS 59371, f. 49; Add. MS 58922, f. 102; H.M.C., *Fortescue*, VIII, 132–3; Add. MS 51593, f. 5.

[12] B.L., Add. MS 34456, ff. 473, 489; Hansard, *Parl. Debs*, VII, 730; Add. MS 58924, f. 76.

[13] B.L., Add. MS 69065, 1 Mar. 1792 (unfoliated); Add. MS 69046, f. 52.

seven days the new measure passed both houses of parliament.¹⁴ These and other instances highlight the fact that Grenville had assumed a leading voice in the Lords' legislative deliberations which formerly were dominated by lawyers such as Mansfield and Thurlow.

As long as he was a minister of the crown as well as leader of the House, Grenville endeavored successfully to maintain a harmonious working relationship with the Commons and, at the same time to uphold the Lords' privileges and rights as a legislative chamber. In 1806 that relationship was temporarily disrupted when the lower chamber summoned Lord Teignmouth, an Irish peer without a seat in the Lords, to appear to give evidence. This summons provoked a semantic debate between the two Houses, as the Lords, spurred on by the earl of Limerick, insisted that the Commons could only request, not demand a peer's attendance. For its part the lower House claimed that because Teignmouth did not enjoy the privilege of parliament, the Commons was entitled to issue the summons. Faced with a new point of protocol and the persistence of Speaker Abbot in upholding the Commons' rights, Grenville confessed 'I know not what part to take in it [the dispute] except that a minister naturally wishes to prevent a dispute between the two Houses, by which Govt is usually the sufferer'. The matter dropped after the Lords adopted a resolution upholding the privileges of all Irish peers. Throughout the 1790s Grenville consulted with Pitt on the construction of bills introduced in the Lords to insure they did not contain clauses that challenged the Commons' privileges regarding money bills. When the Lords did make alterations in such measures the subsequent procedure was usually simple: thus, Speaker Abbot agreed with Grenville as to the wisdom of an amendment in the Lords to an Irish bill regulating charities, adding that the Commons, after rejecting the amended measure, would bring in a new bill incorporating that alteration. In a similar case in 1794, Speaker Addington acknowledged Grenville's superior expertise and deferred to him on how to proceed with an amendment made in the Lords to a bill on contested elections.¹⁵

Even before Grenville took his seat in the house of lords, he had the chance to witness first hand the deficiencies of the Scottish representative peerage system. As home secretary in 1790, he worked with Henry Dundas, the Scottish manager, to secure the largest possible number of government supporters at the hotly contested peerage election. The 16 representatives of the Scottish peerage had to secure election at each new parliament. Normally these contests were sedate affairs at which the government secured the election of most, if not all of its slate. The 1790 election was unusual because of the numerical strength and effective organization of opposition forces. Working in concert with Dundas who had proceeded to Edinburgh, Grenville scoured England for potential supporters. In desperation, Dundas even suggested that

---

[14] B.L., Add. MS 58916, ff. 163–4; Add. MS 58991, f. 157; Add. MS 58924, f. 133; H.M.C., *Fortescue*, VIII, 72–3; Add. MS 59367, ff, 25, 55, 59–60; *The Diary and Correspondence of Charles Abbot, Lord Colchester*, ed. Charles, Lord Colchester (3 vols, 1861), I, 213–5.

[15] B.L., Add. MS 58954, ff. 8, 18; *Colchester Diary*, ed. Colchester, II, 70–3; *Morning Chronicle*, 9, 15, 18 July; *L.J.*, XLV, 807–8; B.L., Add. MS 58907, f. 116; Add. MS 69066, 2 June 1794 (unfoliated). In opposition he was a more aggressive in upholding the privileges of the Lords; in particular, he attacked the Commons' tendency to attach superfluous items to money bills and, in certain instances, to claim exclusive rights to make grants. Hansard, *Parl. Debs*, X, 1079, 1152–3; B.L., Add. MS 58979, f. 66; Durham University Library, Grey MSS, GRE/B21/2/168.

government bribe the impoverished Lord Bellenden with 20 guineas and a bottle of brandy; 'it is not a business for a Secretary of State to be concerned in, but there are such instruments to be employed when such Blackguards are to be dealt with', he added. Grenville rejected this suggestion. However, because the government was able to elect only nine of its supporters, he at once set out to re-establish its hold over peerage contests by upholding the right of Scots peers with British titles to vote in them.[16] He pursued this matter as leader and cajoled the House into adopting his proposal in 1793. Still, he did not aspire like some of his predecessors to manage subsequent elections: Dundas took on that chore in 1796, and in 1806 Grenville left the matter to Lord Spencer, the home secretary, and Lord Moira, the commander in chief in Scotland.

Nevertheless, his experience during and after the Scottish peerage election of 1790 as well as his desire to secure the largest possible following for government shaped the plan he drafted for an Irish representative peerage in 1800. Despite the objections to electing peers to a role that formerly was theirs by right, Grenville pressed for a representative system: the imperial house of lords could not absorb the entire Irish peerage, some of whose members were unqualified either by circumstances or situation for a seat there; on the other hand, it was neither just nor feasible to disenfranchise the entire group.[17] According to Grenville's plan the Irish representative peers, having secured election, would sit for life, thus avoiding the recurring election of over 40 Scots and Irish peers to the hereditary chamber every six or seven years. From the outset Irish nobles with British titles enjoyed the right to vote in peerage elections, a privilege Grenville had earlier secured for their Scottish counterparts; also, in the event an Irish representative peer received a United Kingdom peerage, he retained that seat as well, thus reducing the number of contests. The Act of Union enabled the king to create a new Irish peer for every three extinctions in the Irish nobility; in the event that the number of Irish peers dropped to 100, the crown could replace each subsequent extinct peerage.

Grenville defended his plan against critics in both parliaments. The system, he argued, was 'much better arranged with a view to the permanent interest of the Country than in the Case of Scotland', both because the Irish peers sat for life and because the crown could replenish the order's ranks as existing titles died out. The latter proviso insured that there would always be a choice at Irish peerage elections, thereby precluding the election of persons 'of very low stations in life, and of circumstance extremely below the level of Peerage' – a possibility that existed among the Scottish peerage because of the group's declining numbers. By maintaining the size of the Irish nobility, the act might also help to preclude the 'intrigue and cabal' that, as Grenville knew only too well, characterized some Scottish peerage elections, contests that were all the more tumultuous because of their occurrence every six or seven years.[18]

---

[16] B.L., Add. MS 59258, ff. 7–13, 31–4, 91–2; *L.J.*, XXXIX, 639; J. Debrett, *Parliamentary Register*, 2nd ser., XXXVI, 212–3, 226.

[17] H.M.C., *Fortescue*, VI, 205–6; William R. Perkins Library, Duke University, Bligh Papers: Grenville to Darnley, 24 Apr. 1800. See also Jupp, *Grenville*, pp. 267–9.

[18] B.L., Add. MS 70927, ff. 63–4; Add. MS. 59255, ff. 51–2; Perkins Library, Bligh Papers: Grenville to Darnely, 24 Apr. 1800.

Finally, to fulfill Pitt's mandate of establishing the government position in the house of lords on a new, stronger footing, Grenville provided the reliable, authoritative voice government had hitherto lacked there. Prior to his elevation, the leader might organize followers and potential speakers for an upcoming encounter but had no special responsibility to lead the debates themselves: rather the task of explaining and defending the ministerial position in any given instance usually fell to the chancellor and the responsible minister if he sat in the House. Grenville added an important new dimension to the role of leader: between 1790 and 1801 he presented the government's position on virtually all major business. His own mastery contrasted favourably not only with his weak predecessors but also with the vague or bombastic generalizations of opposition speakers, and he could be dismissive of their arguments. For example, Lord Glenbervie admired his treatment of Lord Holland's somewhat petulant maiden speech: 'on that thoughtless defence, Lord Grenville grounded a very pointed part of the only eloquent speech delivered in a dull debate'. If in the occasionally stultifying atmosphere of the upper chamber he sometimes tended to lecture rather than persuade, he was, at his best, succinct, knowledgeable and convincing. He could also lay out complex issues clearly and in great detail; his presentation of the resolutions for an Irish union, for example, went on for four hours. Not surprisingly, observers were soon extolling his 'most brilliant and commanding talents'; Auckland praised his contribution on 17 February 1794 as one of the 'best speeches that I ever heard in either House of Parliament and delivered with a wonderful promptitude, method and animation'. His performances were all the more impressive because of their frequency and because he often defended the government without assistance from his fellow ministers. In 1797, Grenville explained to his brother that because of the chancellor's indisposition, he would have to answer Lord Moira's criticisms of the government's treatment of Ireland, noting in the process that 'it is not the first time ... and most probably it will not be the last', he was required to take on the whole burden of debate.[19]

To some degree Grenville's achievements as leader were a measure of his own mastery and authority. Even in opposition, he remained the most formidable figure in the House. Anticipating the opening of parliament in the fall of 1801, Hawkesbury, the home secretary, worried that the ministry had no one 'capable of answering Lord Grenville, at least in the manner in which he should be answered'. This concern proved well-founded; Lord Limerick, who seconded the address for the administration at the opening of the session, later described Grenville's response as 'one of the most impressive and powerful speeches I ever heard'. A year later, George Tierney reported that Grenville still dominated the upper chamber: 'the Lords Pelham & Hobart seem to feel themselves out of the question, and the Chancellor is not a match for his noble opponent'.[20] Indeed, it is a measure of Grenville's achievement as leader that after watching the hapless struggles of two floundering leaders – Lords Pelham and Hobart – Addington dispatched Lord Hawkesbury to take command of

---

[19] *Glenbervie Diaries*, ed. Bickley, I, 142; McCahill, *Order and Equipoise*, pp. 137–8, 141; Jupp, *Grenville*, p. 129; *Auckland Correspondence*, ed. Bath and Wells, III, 186; *Courts and Cabinets*, ed. Buckingham, II, 266.

[20] B.L., Add. MS 38235, f. 274; *Colchester Diary*, ed. Colchester, I, 386; Add. MS 51585, ff. 31–3. According to George III Grenville wrote out his speeches in advance but did not try to memorize what he had written. *Glenbervie Diaries*, ed. Bickley, I, 326.

ministerial forces in the Lords at the end of 1803. Though far more effective than his predecessors, Hawkesbury was initially no match for Grenville, as Lord King explained to his friend, Lord Holland:

> I suppose you have heard that Ld Hawkesbury is brought into the H of Lds to make head agt Lord Grenville who never loses an opportunity of discharging his heavy ordnance agt their feeble works. He made one of the best speeches I ever heard on the Bank bill ... it was near two hours long ... He always puts me in a mind of an Iron rail way driving straight forward without friction or impediment.

As late as 1808, Glenbervie reported that the Portland administration was seeking the assistance of Lord Melville because it doubted Hawkesbury could handle both Grenville and Lord Grey.[21] Nevertheless, Hawkesbury grew into the role, ultimately assuming the overall responsibility for the conduct of public business in the House and for the maintenance of a strong administration majority there. Indeed, his powerful presence for so many years as the Lords' leader (as earl of Liverpool) is the best testament to the to the degree that Grenville had enlarged and transformed the post. Once he had established the leadership in the Lords on a new, extended basis, it was impossible to go back to what had existed prior to his elevation: the post demanded not a Hobart or a Pelham but a peer of the first political rank – a Liverpool, a Wellington or a Grey.

Though Grenville dominated the house of lords after 1790, it was only after he moved into opposition that he began to build a party of followers there. Following Pitt's resignation in 1801 Lord Fitzwilliam was surprised to discover 'Ld Grenville without a following where he had been leading so many years and with so great authority'. As spokesman for his cousin's government he attracted no body of personal supporters. However, first as critic of Addington's peace, then as a proponent of catholic emancipation and free trade Grenville rallied a growing group of adherents. The nucleus of his following included family members and old whigs who favored an active prosecution of the war: however, by 1808 the group, which included at least 24 peers, consisted of two parts – those bound to Grenville by personal or familial ties and those bound for ideological reasons.[22]

Despite his discomfort with the notion of systematic opposition, Grenville effectively organized his forces in the Lords. In the five years after the collapse of the talents, he took primary responsibility for devising the timing and tactics of opposition campaigns there. Both whigs and his own followers checked dutifully on the scheduling and content of their motions and even whether those motions were appropriate or timely. He also worked to secure attendances with his own surrogate, Lord Auckland, and with Albemarle, the whig whip. Partly as the result of that organization the opposition gained sufficient numerical strength and credibility in debate to pose a challenge to government forces in the upper house in 1804 and

---

[21] B.L., Add. MS 51572, ff. 63–4; *Glenbervie Diaries*, ed. Bickley, II, 12.

[22] Durham University, Grey MSS., GRE/B14/11/9; J. J. Sack, *The Grenvillites, 1801–29* (Urbana, 1979), p. 132.

again by 1809.[23] From the outset of the alliance he also enjoyed good relations with Fox and Grey, and over time, he strengthened his hold by winning over whigs who had regarded the Grenvillites with initial skepticism. Following Fox's death Lord Chancellor Erskine, who had opposed the junction in 1804, acknowledged that

> I have since had so many opportunities of witnessing the benefits to the public derived from it [the alliance] & the perfect Honor and good faith with which your Lordship has uniformly conducted yourself, and the enlightened views which you have publicly taken of our best national interests, that I place the utmost confidence in you and look forward with certainty to the administration's being in fact & in public opinion *one body*, out of the reach of Malice & intrigue of its enemies.

A year later, Lord Holland, another early sceptic, urged Grenville to come up to London because 'your appearance in the Hse of Lds & any part you take in opposition keep up people's attention to politicks'.[24]

In these circumstances Grenville came to serve as the principal opposition spokesman in the upper House. He spoke forcefully on behalf of issues that united the whigs with his group, most notably catholic emancipation. Friends as well as opponents complained of the persistence and warmth of his defense of emancipation; even Grenville acknowledged that on occasion he sometimes expressed himself 'in terms stronger than was likely to be agreeable to the Ministerialists or to Lord Sidmouth's party'.[25] However, over time he focused more closely on a host of economic and commercial issues. For example, he told Lord Wellesley in 1813 that he

> lean[ed] towards much more enlarged maxims of commercial Legislation than have hitherto been prevalent in this Country. Since 1801 I have given much attention to the study of Political Oeconomy as a Science. I had before acted as a Minister too frequently must, more on separate views of detached questions as they arose than on any uniform & general system of commercial Policy.

As he became more committed to the doctrines of Adam Smith, he delivered more speeches on a range of economic issues on which neither his whig allies nor the main body of peers were well versed. Especially after his resignation in 1807 Grenville was the principal opponent in the house of lords of the orders in council, the suspension of cash payments, the monopoly of the East India Company and the corn laws and the chief advocate of free trade and fiscal retrenchment. Some found his disquisitions dull, others pedantic. On the other hand Malthus hailed his 1813 speech on the East

---

[23] B.L., Add. MS 69068, ff. 49–50; Add. MS 58944, ff. 97–8; Add. MS 48242, f. 106; Add. MS 58950, ff. 79–82; Durham University, Grey MSS., GRE/B21/2/90, 91; Add. MS 58925, ff. 157–61, 163, 168. Though he argues the Grenvillite alliance forced whigs to compromise on important matters of principle, Frank O'Gorman acknowledges Grenville's importance as the opposition leader in *The Emergence of the British Two-Party System 1760–1832* (1982), p. 66. Cf. R. W. Davis, 'The House of Lords, the Whigs and Catholic Emancipation, 1806–1829', *Parliamentary History*, XVIII (1999), 24.

[24] L. G. Mitchell, *Charles James Fox* (Oxford, 1992), pp. 216–7; E. A. Smith, *Lord Grey, 1764–1845* (Oxford, 1990), p. 104; B.L., Add. MS 58950, ff. 87–8; Add. MS 58965, ff. 101–2.

[25] *Auckland Correspondence*, ed. Bath and Wells, IV, 309–10.

Indian monopoly as 'brilliant'.[26] His passionate commitment to Smith's principles provided Grenville with the energy and inducement to continue his labours, despite his professed desire for retirement. The result for the House and his fellow peers was a more frequent, intense and intelligent attention to economic and commercial issues than would otherwise have been the case. In this respect he contributed substantially not only to the education of his whig colleagues but to the Lords as a whole.

If Grenville was unable to convince the majority of peers to share his views on a range of commercial and economic matters, he was eventually able to carry the abolition of the slave trade through that chamber. His own support for abolition dated from 1787, and from then until the final passage of the Abolition Bill he worked closely with a number of abolitionists on behalf of the cause. Wilberforce later claimed that Grenville's encouragement was one of the factors that induced him to bring his first Abolition Bill before the house of commons in 1789. Even as its leader, Grenville was unable to forestall the Lords' dilatory inquiry into the trade that anti-abolitionists perpetuated from 1792 to 1794 as a means of postponing a decision on the question. However, in 1799 he worked closely and more successfully with the radical William Smith on a bill to regulate the trade: not only did Grenville rely on the volume of evidence Smith compiled in support of the measure, but he sought out his opinion on the many amendments proposed in the Lords before proceeding to the bill's committee stage. Calling Grenville 'the natural Guardian & Protector of the Bill for the Abolition of the Slave Trade', Wilberforce appealed to him to take charge of that measure when it came up to the Lords in 1804.[27] Two years later Wilberforce transmitted to the new government Grenville headed James Stephen's plan for the abolition of the foreign slave trade. In carrying that measure, which eliminated two-thirds to three-quarters of the British trade, through the House, Grenville relied on arguments provided him by Stephen. He then followed up on the Foreign Slave Trade Bill with a series of resolutions committing each house to support total abolition. Wilberforce worried during the summer of 1806 that Grenville would rely on high duties to achieve abolition. In fact, on 5 November he announced his intention to bring an Abolition Bill into the house of lords at the beginning of the session; shortly thereafter he distributed copies of the measure among cabinet colleagues and abolitionists, seeking their proposed amendments. The measure passed triumphantly through the house of lords in February 1807.[28]

Nothing better illustrates the range and extent of Grenville's authority in the house of lords than the passage of these two measures. If Stephens was the author of the Foreign Slave Trade Bill, Grenville took the lead in drafting the final abolition measure. More importantly, Roger Anstey claimed that the 'political pressure which Grenville did not hesitate to exert' along with abolitionist lobbying were the proximate

[26] B.L., Add. MS 70928, f. 84. Both Jupp and Sack stress the important role Grenville played in educating his whig partners on economic and commercial issues. Jupp, *Grenville*, pp. 445–7; Sack, *Grenvillites*, pp. 155–7.

[27] B.L., Add. MS 69038, ff. 165–6; William R. Perkins Library, Duke University, William Smith Papers: 10 22 June 1799; Add. MS 59305a, ff. 27–30, 33.

[28] The most thorough account of the house of lords' passage of the abolition measures in 1806 and 1807 is in Roger Anstey, *The Atlantic Slave Trade and British Abolition, 1760–1810* (Atlantic Highlands, N.J., 1975), pp. 366–83, 393–400. Bodl., Wilberforce MSS, D13, ff. 220–1; H.M.C., *Fortescue*, VIII, 454–5.

causes for the success of the 1807 bill.[29] This pressure took several different forms. Grenville pressed for full attendances on the Foreign Slave Trade Bill and the abolition resolutions in 1806. As the session extended from May into June, it became more difficult not only to secure attendances but to arrange the disposition of proxies among those few who remained in London. Yet his careful canvassing deflated Hawkesbury and other leading opponents, who had initially promised stiff resistance in committee and at the Foreign Slave Trade Bill's third reading. He also managed to recruit new supporters, including Lord Leicester; after opposing abolition for 20 years, that peer changed his opinion because Grenville promised to press other powers to follow Britain's example.[30] His moving and forceful speeches in defense of the Foreign Slave Trade Bill and then the Abolition Bill along with active canvassing even among political opponents in January and February produced more notable results.

The triumphant passage of the Abolition Bill's second reading by a majority of 100 to 36 represented a dramatic transformation in the Lords' approach to this issue. Eight years earlier 68 peers had combined to defeat Henry Thornton's bill to abolish the trade on the Sierra Leone coast, a measure supported by Pitt but openly opposed by the court and the prince of Wales. By 1806 Fox had neutralized the prince, and early in 1807 Grenville had apparently stifled the court: of the 50 peers who had opposed Thornton's bill and were still active in 1807, four switched sides and supported abolition; another 34 did not vote at the bill's second reading. In 1799 17 courtiers opposed Thornton's bill, but only five voted against the Abolition Bill. Lord Westmorland, a leading opponent of abolition, later complained of the violence with which Grenville forced the measure through the House.[31] That violence not only secured the attendance of supporters; it deterred many who may have opposed it from voting against the king's minister.

If his canvassing was effective, so were his efforts to check the obstruction of his opponents. Grenville understandably worried that those opposing abolition would resort once again to delaying tactics and demand the interrogation of witnesses. To counter this possibility in 1806 he instructed his deputy, Lord Auckland, to give notice of and set a firm date for the second reading and to resist demands for delay from the duke of Clarence and other opponents. Privately, he made allowances for the possibility that it would be necessary once again to take testimony before the House. Publicly he did all he could to resist such a possibility. Whenever the issue came up in the House, he opposed it.[32] Having carried the Foreign Slave Trade Bill, he then laid out his subsequent strategy in a long letter to Sidmouth, a potential cabinet opponent of abolition: first would come the resolutions, then the measure itself, to be introduced 'at the very opening of the next Session ... so as to put it out of the power of our opponents again to defeat us by the disgraceful methods of delay which have so much hurt the Character of the Ho of Lords'. He agreed to Westmorland's request in January to defer the Abolition Bill's second reading so

---

[29] Jupp, *Grenville*, pp. 389–91; Anstey, *Atlantic Slave Trade*, p. 398.
[30] H.M.C., *Fortescue*, VIII, 133 139–40; B.L., Add. MS 58964, f. 33.
[31] For the Lords' division list on Thornton's Bill, see *Later Correspondence of George III*, ed. Aspinall, III, 226–8; P.R.O., 30/8/369, ff. 291–2.
[32] H.H.C., *Fortescue*, VIII, 133, 138; Hansard, *Parl. Debs*, VIII, 257–8, 601–2, 613–4, 617.

its opponents could muster their supporters and marshal their case. As he did so, he told Wilberforce that he would resist all efforts for further inquiries, and he privately warned Clarence that supporters of abolition would force a division on the issue if it came up in the House. In the end, opponents declined to call for more evidence.[33]

By 1806 the issue for Grenville was no longer whether abolition was right or just; that case had long since been established. Rather the central question was whether the house of lords could overcome the ignominy of its past conduct. As he neared the end of his great speech in support of the Abolition Bill's second reading on 5 February, he exhorted the House at last to redeem itself:

> in calling your attention to this great measure, let me entreat you to consider that the whole country looks to the parliament to wipe away the stigma attached to its character in continuing this detestable traffic; that it looks not merely to parliament, but to your lordships' house. Twice has this measure failed in this house, and if this iniquitous traffic is not now abolished, the guilt will rest with your lordships.[34]

This argument was as powerful as it was uncomfortable for the house of lords, and to a degree contradicts the argument of historians who claim that the upper chamber carried the measure amidst an orgy of self-congratulation. In fact, this speech only represented the culmination of his admonitions over the past eight years in which he had condemned the Lords' delaying tactics. More importantly, it powerfully reflects the degree to which the leading figure in the house of lords believed that the institution put itself in a vulnerable position by condoning and perpetuating an evil that was clearly perceived and broadly condemned by a substantial section of the public.

The arguments Grenville used before the House to a degree challenge his biographer's complaint that he refused to grant 'a positive role to public opinion in the governing process'. In a recent article Professor Richard Davis argues that Grenville accepted that there was such a thing as public opinion to which he and other politicians had to pay heed.[35] Throughout the debates first on the regulation and then the abolition of the slave trade, peers had cited popular support as one reason for the House to proceed. Grenville extended their argument. 'The whole country' he told his listeners in 1807 waited on the outcome of their deliberations. More importantly, he alone among leading abolitionists in the House directly condemned the Lords for its willingness to condone the delaying tactics of the measure's opponents, thus prolonging what he and popular opinion decried as an immoral, unpardonable traffic. His conduct in the House on the abolition issue is notable because of his argument that the Lords could not indefinitely thwart a cause which had gained clear moral and popular ascendancy. As the oligarchic politics of the eighteenth century gave way to a more open and popular political environment, Grenville was the first major figure in the house of lords not only to deliver this message there but to act forcefully upon it.

---

[33] H.M.C., *Fortescue*, VIII, 168–70; B.L., Add. MS 58305a, ff. 128, 130; Add. MS 58976, f. 92; Add. MS 58869, ff. 205, 207.

[34] Hansard, *Parl. Debs*, VIII, 663.

[35] Jupp, *Grenville*, p. 468; Davis, 'Catholic Emancipation', pp. 25–9.

Wellington*

RICHARD W. DAVIS

In the autumn of 1831, shortly after the house of lords had thrown out the Reform Bill on its second reading, Marquess Wellesley remarked to Lord Holland: 'There never was a more crafty villain than my brother Arthur.' The marquess can hardly be accused of showing undue partiality to his sibling; but there was also impeccably whig testimony to the same effect. George Lamb said of the duke of Wellington: 'He is so d—d cunning. People don't know him, he is the cunningest fellow in the world.'[1]

The duke's craftiness and cunningness can doubtless be exaggerated, perhaps especially in his handling of the issue of parliamentary reform. Historians, however, have generally failed to recognize any trace of these qualities in Wellington. He is usually portrayed as he portrayed himself: as a blunt, straightforward, no-nonsense kind of old soldier, always speaking his mind frankly, sometimes perhaps with too much irascibility, but at bottom with bluff good will for all. Had Wellington been the man he pretended to be, he would have been a complete disaster as a politician. In fact, however, though he possessed all the above qualities, and often deployed them with great skill, he was not the man he pretended to be. He was a shrewd and skillful politician. Like all politicians, he had his failures, some of them large. But he also had his successes, most especially in the way in which he steered the house of lords through the stormy waters of post-reform politics and into a secure berth at last in the new political system.[2] Had he failed, nineteenth-century Britain would have been a different kind of place, and probably not a better one. Wellington's political career, especially the leading part he played in the house of lords, has never been seriously studied. It needs to be.

The 1820s was the last decade in which the house of lords saw itself primarily as a loyal bastion of support for the monarch. The Lords, it is true, could never be taken for granted, nor was it; still the upper House continued to proceed on the assumption that its primary function was to provide a reliable bulwark for the crown, as it had for the past century and more. It followed that the monarch's support of a government remained crucial for its smooth functioning in the Lords, even though

---

* I am indebted to the archival staffs of Southampton University, Nottingham University and the Henry E. Huntington Library for much care and attention while I worked for extended periods in papers under their charge. I am also grateful to the controller of Her Majesty's Stationery Office for permission to include Crown Copyright material from the Wellington papers.

[1] *The Holland House Diaries, 1831–1840*, ed. A. D. Kriegel (1977), p. 85.

[2] See *Lords of Parliament. Studies, 1714–1914*, ed. R. W. Davis (Stanford, 1995), ch. 6.

by this time that support was based more on sentiment than on the practical interest once provided by patronage.[3]

After 1830 when Wellington's government went out of office the attitude and position of the Lords swiftly changed. It did not take the duke long, as leader of the opposition, to decide that the machinery for the elections of 16 Scottish and 28 Irish representative peers which he had controlled as prime minister, he could and should continue to control out of office. The result was to transfer a large block of heretofore government patronage to the Conservative party and its leader in the house of lords. This accession of patronage, combined with a growing conservatism among the peerage after the Reform Act, made the upper House for most of the rest of the century a fairly safe preserve of that party – some would, and did say, a mere tool of the party in the manner of 'Mr. Balfour's poodle'. Yet, as Wellington knew from the beginning and Balfour's own experience would soon prove, an upper House which conducted itself merely as an instrument of partisan politics would soon be in serious trouble. The Parliament Act of 1911 gave the poodle a drastic trimming.

Though Wellington began regular attendance in the house of lords in 1819, his impact upon it was for some time not great. He spoke infrequently, mostly on military and diplomatic matters, and rarely at much length. From among former colleagues in the army and diplomacy and others with older social and political connexions, there probably would have been a nucleus in the Lords for some kind of Wellington party; but so long as the earl of Liverpool retained his health and vigour, the duke's allegiance to him was firm and unwavering.

The ease and speed with which Wellington made the transition from follower to leader was amazing. The duke himself was still bemused with his luck two decades later, at the end of an eventful political career. As he admitted to Lord Stanley in February 1846: 'it is not easy to account for my being in the situation that I have so long filled in the House of Lords. Its commencement was very accidental.' At the beginning of 1827, he was, as he had been since 1818, master general of the ordnance with a seat in the cabinet. Within a year he would be prime minister. What altered his situation was Liverpool's incapacitating stroke. 'I at once succeeded to the exercise of the influence and power that he had for many years exercised in the House of Lords always in high office, which however unworthy I have held ever since whether in or out of office.'[4]

The facts were as the duke stated them; but a little more explanation is possible. That Liverpool's mantle had fallen on his shoulders, Wellington demonstrated in early June 1827 when he carried what Viscount Goderich, the official leader of the Lords in Canning's government, warned would be a wrecking amendment to a long-awaited corn bill. Wellington denied that it was his intention to wreck the bill, and held that his amendment should not have done so. The nature of the amendment was sufficiently technical not to commit him for the future, and his government would carry a bill the following year; but for the time being it brought him the support of the old tories, and made him the leader of a majority in the House. As the

---

[3] D. Large, 'The Decline of "the Party of the Crown" and the Rise of Parties in the Lords, 1783–1837', *English Historical Review*, LXXVIII (1963), 669–95.

[4] Southampton University Library, Wellington Papers, WP2/138/41–4.

duke of Buckingham remarked: 'The government must go or strengthen itself.'[5] The government, which Goderich would lead after Canning's death, would never meet parliament again.

Yet, having taken this decisive step, Wellington soon took another, which appeared equally decisive in the opposite direction. He agreed to resume the office of commander-in-chief of the army, which, as he cheerfully admitted to Lord Eldon meant, so far as the government was concerned that 'I can be of no council or party against them.' His new followers seem not to have been unduly alarmed by this turn of events, and, as it turned out they were right, for by 2 January 1828, a week before he was invited to form a government, Wellington was busy, with the help of Lords Bathurst and Melville and the apparent connivance of Lord Chancellor Lyndhurst, rallying peers to attend the opening of parliament and planning a dead set against the government's foreign policy.[6] Commander-in-chief or not, the duke of Wellington was acting very much like a party leader.

Conveniently provided with the king's commands, Wellington set about forming his government, and then soon faced the problems of controlling it and of maintaining a majority in the two houses of parliament, which in the Lords was his own personal responsibility. The major elements in the machinery for managing the Lords were already in place. Before each session of parliament, the leader of the House sent a letter to all peers believed to be favourable to the government, asking for their attendance, or in lieu of that at least a valid proxy. Identifying such peers and keeping the lists up to date was primarily the responsibility of the whip, though Wellington gave the lists an annual scrutiny. In order to give a proxy, a lord had, of course, to have taken his seat. Having done so, he was entitled to give proxies for the remainder of that parliament; but proxies had to be renewed in each session, and any time he appeared in person thereafter the proxy was rendered invalid and a new one had to be secured. Keeping track of the peers and their proxies was no mean task for the whip; but it was a highly important one. Governments were usually well ahead of the opposition in the proxies they held, and not infrequently the latter made the difference between victory and defeat. The government's advantage lay at least partly in its superior organization. The latter was not large. Usually all the tasks were handled by, at most, the leader, the whip, and one or two of Wellington's secretaries, sometimes with extra help brought in to transcribe letters. What gave government the edge was that all those concerned were rewarded in some tangible fashion for doing the job.

In addition to this skeletal organization, there were partly social functions which were rapidly being transmogrified into minor political institutions. The dinner given by the leader at the beginning of the session had been a familiar practice for some time. Since Liverpool's coming to power in 1812, it had, on what became the tory side, been given by the prime minister, providing an occasion for a reading of the king's speech and a general discussion of policy.

---

[5] Hansard, *Parl. Debs*, new ser., XVII, 1096–8, 1223; Henry E. Huntington Library, STG 98: diary of the first duke of Buckingham, 3 and 6 June 1827.

[6] Southampton U.L., WP1/898/1: copy Wellington to Eldon, 1 Sep. 1827; 897/1: Londonderry to Wellington, n.d. [Sept. 1827]; 913/9: Melville to Wellington, 8 Jan. 1828; H.M.C., *Bathurst*, p. 650.

Wellington duly followed this precedent during his premiership, but had no idea of following it thereafter. The ultra tory peers thought otherwise, and early in 1831 began to demand that there be meetings and consultations. The situation was complicated by the fact that the rupture between Wellington and the ultras over catholic emancipation remained an open one, with the result that neither had an overpowering desire to meet the other. The duke of Buckingham and the marquess of Londonderry who were now moving towards the ultras, in large part for their own purposes, saw advantages in perpetuating the breach, hoping it would allow them to bring ultras and moderates together, in the process squeezing out Wellington and Sir Robert Peel. But the ultras were not to be thus seduced. They hankered for a reconciliation with their former leaders, a hankering which grew as the reform crisis deepened. Wellington too was willing to let bygones be bygones. He still had no desire for meetings, and aided by the excuse that he was in mourning for his duchess, he managed to avoid those to which the ultras tried to entice him. He told Bathurst about one to be held at the earl of Mansfield's to concert policy on reform that he wanted to stay away from it because it would not do any good, adding 'But it is well to avoid any argument on the subject.'[7]

Wellington believed that there was no good to be gained by large party meetings; that they would probably create more divisions than they bridged; and that besides over-exciting those attending, they were likely to raise fears in their opponents. His ruses to avoid political entertaining were ludicrous. He claimed that no more than 50 people could dine at Apsley House, whereas the Waterloo Gallery could accommodate at least twice that many. And after the Reform Act, in his desire to keep the Lords quiet for as long as possible into the session, he would disappear from London after the debate on the address and remain away most of the time until after Easter. The meetings, however, grew more, not less. By 1838 the duke had changed his tune. In response to a plea from the whip, Lord Redesdale, Wellington replied early in January that he could quite 'understand lords wishing to have a meeting; and I will go to town either tomorrow or next day; and will immediately fix one'. And by 1840 he was cheerfully offering not one, but two dinners at the beginning of the session – with 50 at each, 'though the number is greater than is convenient'.[8] The reasons for his change of heart are not far to seek. In the first place, one of his concerns about meetings in the period of acute tensions between the two Houses after 1831 had disappeared by 1834, when the tory cause once more began to prosper. The second reason was that, contrary to the duke's expectations, meetings proved to be an effective way to keep his followers happy and together.

The years of the reform debates were unusual ones, without much sign of organization. The duke did call meetings on occasion, but so far as he was able small ones. In late September 1831 he had 16 peers to dinner at Apsley House to decide on accepting Lord Eldon's policy of meeting the Reform Bill itself with a decided rejection, but with no commitments against any or all reform proposals beyond the

---

[7] Huntington Lib., STG 85(10): Londonderry to Buckingham, 25 Jan. 1831; Southampton U.L., WP1/1186/25: copy Wellington to Bathurst, 26 May 1831.

[8] Gloucestershire R.O., D2002 (Redesdale MSS.), 5/1/2: Wellington to Redesdale, 28 Jan. 1838, and same to same, 6 Jan. 1840.

specific one before them. Those invited were peers the duke reckoned to be the 'principal opponents of the bill' and among them were 'men of all parties'. But he explained to Earl De la Warr that, considering 'the jealousy and suspicion attached to every movement of the members of the House of Lords, we have thought it best not to have a general meeting of the opponents of the measure'.[9]

Because of ultra discontent with Wellington's actions over the passage of the Reform Bill in May 1832, especially his leading a massive tory abstention which allowed it to pass the Lords, the following year also began badly, and got worse, because of violent differences of opinion over the whig government's Irish Church Bill, which abolished bishoprics, redistributed the Church's resources, and threatened lay appropriation. Occasionally Wellington did something his critics could applaud. Early in the consideration of the issue he showed the cunningness noticed by his contemporaries. For reasons that were not immediately apparent, he chose this time to challenge in the Lords the government's very liberally inclined neutrality in the contest between liberal and conservative factions in Portugal, and roundly defeated Grey and his colleagues. The government, at least, got the message and a couple of weeks later the tories were able to rejoice when it dropped the hated clause on appropriation.[10] In the interim, the ultra duke of Newcastle was greatly encouraged when, on 14 June, he dined at Apsley House: 'I mention it because it was evidently an attempt to get all shades of conservatives together, which is most important.'[11] Unfortunately, however, this did not mean what Newcastle hoped, that Wellington would wage all-out war on the bill; for he had early been advised by the primate of Ireland that the Church was in a desperate state and, bad though the bill was, must accept what it offered in the way of relief. The ultras were determined that the bill would be defeated on the second reading. Wellington was equally determined that it would not be. And on the day, as the vote approached, he made sure by rising, and surrounded by his 'particular friends', ostentatiously leaving the House. This left the ultras at the mercy of the whigs: the second reading was carried by 157 to 98. Wellington followed this procedure not once but three times in the course of the bill's final passage.[12]

Wellington here demonstrated that, as the whig ministers would soon be able to rely on those who were now called the conservatives to keep their radical followers in check, so the conservative leader in the Lords would not hesitate to use the whigs to keep his ultra followers in line. That message was delivered with resounding force in the summer of 1833. In one sense this certainly strengthened Wellington's position as leader. On the other hand, the fact that 98 lords, or about 50 per cent of a Conservative party of around 200, were prepared to defy their leader, would very much have tempered any inclinations toward triumphalism Wellington might have had.[13] So far as one can tell, he had none. He had shown that he possessed a powerful weapon, but he was not foolish enough to believe that it could be used too often.

---

[9] Southampton U.L., WP1/1196/2: Wellington's draft reply written on a letter of duke of Northumberland to Wellington, 22 Sep. 1831; /12: copy Wellington to De la Warr, 26 Sept. 1831.

[10] *Lords of Parliament*, ed. Davis, pp. 105–6.

[11] Nottingham University Library, Newcastle MSS. no. 2: diaries of the fourth duke, Ne 2F 4/1, p. 223.

[12] *Ibid.*, pp. 237, 238, 240.

[13] In R. W. Davis, 'The Duke of Wellington and the Ultra Peers', *Wellington Studies III*, ed. C. M. Woolgar (Southampton, 1999), 42–3, I estimated those of ultra sentiments in 1833 as being

No dinners were proffered at the beginning of the 1834 session, but the ultras soon found other more solid grounds for satisfaction with Wellington. In the summer of 1835, Lord Holland, a shrewd and perceptive observer of the duke, noticed that he began to indulge in a more decided tone of 'High Church politics' and set the example to his colleagues in 'high Orange and Protestant language'; but Holland inclined to the explanation of others who knew the duke well that 'such compliance with the prejudices of the more wrongheaded of his party is one of his *straight forward* manoeuvres for acquiring authority and thereby checking the impatience of his unruly types'.[14] Wellington had pursued a very similar line in the early months of the previous year, though then he had begun with opposition to dissenting demands for admission to the ancient universities, gone on to oppose Jewish emancipation, and ended with throwing out a Tithe Bill which went too far in meeting the demands of Irish catholics. In short in 1834 he had performed the whole ultra repertoire. The performance was appreciated. In April, Lord Londonderry remarked with relish: 'The Duke of Wellington is decidedly more *blooded* this session than he was last.' Londonderry attributed the new spirit to Wellington's election as chancellor of Oxford University, which probably strengthened the latter's position in the Lords; though it was deeply resented by Peel, which was to complicate Wellington's and the Lords' relations with the Conservatives in the Commons the next year. Peel probably had another cause for complaint against the duke. In response to Lord Aberdeen, who often served as an intermediary between the two, as to why there had been no attempt to amend the Tithe Bill in a committee stage after a second reading, Wellington replied: 'I could not have commanded our majority if I had allowed the second reading to pass unopposed ... The Conservative majority in the House of Lords would have been lost; at least would not have been under my direction.'[15] There were times when it was advisable to ride with a loose rein.

Towards the end of the 1834 session, however, Newcastle acknowledged Wellington's uniquely powerful position: 'On whichever side the Duke of Wellington is, a majority is sure. If he opposes a measure he is supported, if the next he support it, the majority will follow him.'[16] Later that year the whigs would be dismissed by the king, now William IV, and Wellington would hold the ring for Peel to return from Italy and form a government. Besides being foreign secretary, Wellington would also be leader of the House in this government. But there was not a great deal of leading to be done. The ultras were too happy at being in power to make any trouble, and the life of the ministry was over before there was much serious business for the Lords to do.

What followed was what one contemporary and some historians have seen as the most serious crisis of the duke's political career when, in the midst of violent

---

[13] (*continued*) 70 percent of the party. This was based on Lord Londonderry's reference in September 1835 to 'Out of 140 of our party in the House only 60 today ...'. Lists that I have subsequently found, however, both before and after, put party strength at about 200 in this decade. This suggests that Londonderry must have been referring to those peers still in London and available for service. The number seems large, especially for September, but the municipal corporations bill was still being hotly contested.

[14] *Lords of Parliament*, ed. Davis, p. 104.

[15] Davis, 'Wellington and the Ultra Peers', pp. 46–7.

[16] Nottingham Univ. Lib., Ne 2F 4/1, p. 295.

disagreements in the Conservative party over the Municipal Corporations Bill, he was allegedly displaced and supplanted as leader of the party in the Lords by Lord Lyndhurst. Disraeli was the originator of this yarn, and as in many other similar instances he considerably embellished the truth. The truth is that Wellington was seriously torn on the issue, pulled by his own deep detestation of the bill as a piece of dangerous democratic experimentation, on the one hand, and by his loyalty to the new leader of his party, on the other; for Peel supported the measure. The majority of the duke's conservative colleagues in the Lords ardently shared his own personal bias. Unfortunately, it was one on which he felt unable to act. But neither was he sure that loyalty to Peel was fully warranted in this matter; for the duke had a genuine admiration for, and, more unusual, even trust in Lyndhurst, and the latter's violent opposition to the bill made him doubt his own instinct here too. As a result throughout the crisis Wellington's actions were more characterized by caution than decisiveness. In fact, this approach happened to be the right one to avoid what might have been a disastrous sundering of the new Conservative party a decade before such an event actually occurred.

After adjourning on 13 April 1835, after the fall of Peel's government, parliament met again on 12 May. On 15 July the Conservative lords were invited to Apsley House, where Wellington apprised them of the imminent arrival in their House of important legislation, the Municipal Corporations Bill and another Irish Tithe Bill, and advised them that because all the important business would be done in committee, where proxies did not count, personal attendance would be vital. That is, he told them that these bills should be passed, with as much useful revision as they could accomplish. It was the Corporation Bill that drew fire. Westmorland, one of Wellington's most loyal friends, began with a strong dissent to the idea of the bill's passing. Wellington replied that 'it was open to discussion of course, but that it must proceed as our friends in the House of Commons had acknowledged the principle of interference and lent themselves to amending it in committee'. Then followed an onslaught from all sides, with no peer wholly in favour of the bill. At the meeting's close, as Newcastle recorded, Wellington claimed to see 'much good in [the discussion] and said it might be that before we take the Bill into consideration that he would ask our attendance when we might consider the nature of the Bill and what course it would be most proper to pursue'.[17]

The second meeting at Apsley House took place on 27 July. Wellington there advised a gathering of 70 or 80 peers that they should pass the second reading. According to Newcastle, all present agreed, with one exception (besides Newcastle himself, of course), the earl of Mansfield, a leading ultra, 'who however agreed more than I liked'.[18]

The following day in the Lords, Viscount Strangford moved that petitioners against the bill be heard by counsel at the bar of the House. Viscount Melbourne, the prime minister, objected that this would delay the second reading of the bill; whereupon Wellington suggested that counsel be heard after the second reading, but before going into committee, which was generally agreed upon. Two counsel were duly heard

[17] *Ibid.*, F5/1, pp. 43–6.
[18] *Ibid.*, pp. 48–9.

on 1 August, and Melbourne thereupon moved an adjournment until the following Monday, when the House would go into committee on the bill. Newcastle enquired whether this meant that Melbourne did not intend to allow evidence to be heard in support of counsel, to which the curt reply was that it certainly did. This set Newcastle off on a violent attack on the bill and its sponsor. The bill proposed a vast and arbitrary confiscation of property. It was therefore unconstitutional, and the prime minister deserved to be impeached, which Newcastle would be happy to undertake. No one else followed the duke to such extremes; but Lords Falmouth and Lyndhurst pursued the question of evidence, without any decision being taken.[19]

Evidence, however, was foremost in the minds of most who attended a large meeting at Apsley House on the morning of the day the committee stage of the bill was to begin, 3 August. Wellington advised proceeding with the committee, and did his best to resist the call for further evidence. But resistance was in vain, and when Lyndhurst declared that he intended to vote for evidence being produced, Wellington gave way and agreed to do the same.

Proceedings in the House were both confused and acrimonious. Melbourne was prevented from moving the committee by the earl of Carnarvon's motion for evidence. Lord Winchilsea made some inflammatory remarks, but the day was Lyndhurst's. In a long speech, he dissected the bill clause by clause, demolishing each one. He too stressed the threat to property. But he ended by dismissing the bill as a mere 'party job', aimed at bolstering the whigs and weakening the Conservatives in the country. Wellington, speaking later in the debate, committed himself to no more than supporting Carnarvon's amendment that 'evidence be heard at their Bar before they proceeded further with the Bill'.[20]

It is at this point that Disraeli saw Lyndhurst displacing Wellington as the real leader of the Conservative peers, and others at the time saw it as at least a serious reversal for the duke, at the hands of his followers, if not of Lyndhurst. But this reaction needs to be seen in the context of the duke's previous apparent invincibility. As a matter of fact, this event had little effect on the way Wellington went about leading. From the beginning of the parliamentary discussion, the duke had confined himself to facilitating and conciliating, as in his suggestion of a way to hear counsel, as the Conservative peers wanted, without postponing the second reading, which the government was intent on preventing. In this fashion he continued. In fact, the hearing of evidence was concluded expeditiously, in less than a week. Again, Wellington had gently edged the process along. On Friday, 7 August, the marquess of Salisbury raised the question of whether any more evidence was necessary. This was probably not by chance. Salisbury was an ultra in principle (as indeed was the duke himself), but one who after 1829 usually supported Wellington in a pinch. In Wellington's first dramatic withdrawal just before the vote on the second reading of the Irish Church Bill in 1833, Salisbury was prominently at his side. Some of the comment which followed the marquess's questioning whether more evidence was needed was not surprisingly in the affirmative. Wellington, however, took the

---

[19] Hansard, *Parl. Debs*, 3rd ser., XXIX, 1132–6, 1338–40.
[20] Huntington Lib., STG 85(36): Londonderry to Buckingham, 3 Aug. 1835; Hansard, *Parl. Debs*, 3rd ser., XXIX, 1342, 1393–1401, 1419–21.

occasion to remind the House that the bill must be dealt with before the end of a session fast drawing to a close. He proposed that counsel conclude their evidence at an early hour the next day, and that the House then consider its further proceedings on the bill. This is precisely what happened.[21]

There is no doubt whatever that Lyndhurst served as the manager of the bill in the House, but this hardly made him leader of the party. Whether or not the leader was in office and therefore leader of the House, he did not personally manage every bill. And if any bill ever required a lawyer's management, it was this one. Wellington remained leader of the party in the Lords. The revolt, such as it was, fizzled out within a week. As Lord Fitzgerald reported to Peel, who was in Staffordshire, at a meeting of a hundred Conservative peers at Apsley House on 10 August, the duke strongly expressed his wish that the bill be allowed to go into committee. Lyndhurst then outlined the amendments he intended to move in committee, which were 'sufficiently extensive to satisfy those present'. Lord Falmouth was the only '*un*-compromising' peer there. And the duke of Cumberland, the king's brother and an ultra of ultras, actually 'pressed the necessity of union'.[22]

Hereafter the tension was not one between the Conservative lords and their leader, but rather one between the Lords and the leader of the Conservative party. The bad feeling between Peel and Wellington now began to take its toll on party harmony. Peel was furious about what the upper House was doing and that he was not consulted. The fact that he was in Staffordshire would not have made consultation easy, and he made no attempt to contact Wellington directly. Rather he left it to Fitzgerald to inform the duke of his anger over the decision to hear evidence and over the strength of Lyndhurst's attack on the bill. Wellington agreed that the former lord chancellor 'had gone too far in his speech against the principle of the bill, after what had passed in communications with you'. But not least because of Wellington's actions, the passing of the second reading did take place in a timely fashion. The principle of the bill was accepted. Fitzgerald believed that the amendments Lyndhurst then proposed would be too extensive for the government to accept.[23] That, of course, proved to be the case. When the Commons began consideration of the Lords' amendments on 30 August, Lord John Russell speaking for the government, though conciliatory, found fault especially with a clause that proposed that aldermen should serve for life. Peel who now reappeared after almost a month's silence in the country, backed him to the hilt. Since the clause would have put a severe check on the powers of the elected members of the council, Peel's action is from one point of view quite understandable. What is not understandable is how a leader of the Conservative party, who had held himself incommunicado for the entire period of the Lords' consideration of the bill, should now appear suddenly and unannounced to strike down their work with one blow.

Deserted as they were by their leader in the house of commons, Wellington had to advise the conservative lords that they must give way, but he was furious. Peel himself seems to have decided that he had been rather too highhanded. As G. Kitson Clark has remarked, in negotiations the next year over an Irish Corporations Bill, Peel

---

[21] Hansard, *Parl. Debs*, 3rd ser., XXX, 136–7.
[22] B.L., Add. MS 40323, ff. 292–9.
[23] *Ibid*.

demonstrated 'a very nervous and sensitive loyalty to the Lords'.[24] But this is to talk about Peel's leadership. Wellington's was actually most effective in 1835. By exposing himself to meeting after meeting of the peers, and by making tactical concessions, the duke managed to keep his party together, and under his direction most of the time, in a very trying period. He was not at his strongest and most forceful – he had been both over the Irish Church Bill – but he was at least equally effective. He had thoroughly learned that there was more to leadership than simply to command.

How thoroughly he had learned, and how well he put the lessons into practice, is revealed in an account of a meeting five years later in 1840. Wellington strongly disagreed with the policy of the whig government in proposing to implement Lord Durham's recommendation of a union of the two Canadas. His reservations were mainly on the ground that such a large colony would be much more difficult to control. Though Peel backed the government, Wellington pushed his opposition to the point where there threatened to be a nasty and open split. Once more, on the eve of the second reading of a government bill, there was a proposal for a hearing of evidence, this time in the form of a notice of a motion by the duke himself. But he drew back. He would give up his motion, and he would support going into committee. He would not give up his personal opposition to the government's bill, but would call a meeting of the Conservative peers to explain his own position, but to advise them not to oppose the bill. Lord Aberdeen, who was exercising his diplomatic skills to resolve the disagreement, hoped that the duke would be 'so far successful as to prevent any open division'.

He was successful beyond Aberdeen's most optimistic expectations. 'The effect of his address was like magic; and although we had many present who were obstinate, violent and wrong-headed, not a syllable was said in opposition to the duke's suggestion.' Aberdeen went on to say that 'I have never known such an instance of his power and influence. Under the peculiar circumstances in which this question was placed, that he should only have found ten persons refractory is most wonderful.'[25] Meetings and consultations with his followers, which Wellington had long resisted, had proven one of his greatest sources of strength.

There were others, one of which, the control of the election of Irish representative peers, he had largely inherited from Lord Liverpool. Liverpool's control of those elections may have benefitted from the fact that at the same time he became leader of the Lords in 1804, he also held the office of home secretary, as the home office was in charge of Irish government. Perhaps that was why he was able to take charge immediately of the Irish peerage elections.[26] Certainly, however, no home secretary after him exercised that power. Before Liverpool himself became prime minister two

---

[24] G. Kitson Clark, *Peel and the Conservative Party. A Study in Party Politics, 1832–1841* (1964), p. 347. On pp. 286–93, Kitson Clark seems to suggest that Wellington's leadership continued to be uncertain and insecure even after his victory on going into committee. There were only two party meetings thereafter, one just before Peel made his pronouncement in the Commons, the other just after. At the former the duke advised that the peers should hold their fire until they knew the government's position. At the latter he advised that they should concede, which they did. Lord Fitzgerald, the main source on the party meetings from July on, felt that Wellington should have been stronger and more forthright during the whole period. But unpopular as he himself was in the Lords, Fitzgerald's judgment should not be given too much weight.

[25] *Lords of Parliament*, ed. Davis, pp. 112–13.

[26] B.L., Add. MS. 38241, ff. 49–50.

of those under whom he served, William Pitt and much more egregiously the duke of Portland, made promises they ought not to have made; but afterwards he kept the final decisions in his own hands, and things ran much more smoothly.

It was this system of controlling elections that Wellington inherited when he in turn became prime minister in 1828. His innovation, as has been noticed, was not to give up control when he ceased to be prime minister. Nor did he let it go when Peel formally became the leader of the whole Conservative party after 1834. Here, it must be admitted that Peel was the party sorely tried, though he behaved with tolerant good humour. Naturally in theory the party leader (or, if he happened to be in power the prime minister) was in charge here as elsewhere. Wellington always acted as if this were the case. When a vacancy occurred (once elected, Irish representative peers served for life, so a vacancy could occur at any time), he would submit to Peel a list of possible candidates from which he might choose. If, however, the duke did not get the answer he wanted an elaborate game of manoeuvring began. Early on, he played the earl of Roden, the leader of the Orange party, and Peel off against each other. Of course, he assured Peel, he could have anyone he chose, but Roden certainly represented the majority opinion among the Irish peers who constituted the electorate, and the duke had always found it wise to consult him. Wellington did consult Roden, often invoking Peel as a way of shaping the former's advice.

The most complex and elaborate of these manoeuvres began in 1838, when Roden informed Wellington that Lord De Vesci, the candidate decided on for the next vacancy declined to stand, and suggested instead the very Orange earl of Rathdowne. Wellington advised Peel that Rathdowne would be the most popular candidate, *if*, in fact, De Vesci had determined not to stand. At the same time, the duke suggested that Peel might give De Vesci a little nudge, through the latter's son, an M.P.[27] Much to Roden's amazement and anger De Vesci reversed himself and was duly returned at the next election in January 1839. In the meantime, another Irish peer, Lord Farnham, died. Wellington again informed Peel that Rathdowne would be the most popular choice with the 'old Protestant party', but this time ventured to suggest that the earl of Dunraven, a recent convert from the whigs, would be a more useful choice. Peel agreed to this, but Roden replied, dismissing Dunraven and once more pressing Rathdowne. Apparently without consulting Peel, Wellington wrote back that perhaps Roden would prefer Farnham's son, Roden's brother-in-law. Roden responded that he would be pleased to have his brother-in-law a candidate in future, *after* Rathdowne. Temporarily stymied, Wellington wrote Peel that as Rathdowne was to be the next candidate, perhaps Dunraven, not Farnham should be the candidate after him. But when the next vacancy occurred, in April 1839, Wellington denied to Peel that any firm promise had been made either to Rathdowne or to Roden; Peel, he held, was free to choose any candidate he wanted. As it happened, the candidate decided upon was Dunraven, who was duly elected in September 1839. Wellington had got the man he wanted. But he was not through yet. He was surprised to find that Peel appeared to think that 'as Lord Rathdowne had waived his pretensions to facilitate the election of Lord Dunraven it would be desirable to consider of his claims upon the next vacancy'. Wellington did not think so at all: there were several

[27] B.L., Add. MS. 40310, f. 236.

who had better claims. One of these was Lord Crofton, who Wellington casually mentioned was a 'respectable looking young man of good manners and apparently good inclinations'.[28] Peel did think that Rathdowne had claims, if he pressed them. They had better find out. Barring that, Peel did not think they could do better than Crofton, if Wellington agreed. He did. Peel then read in a Dublin newspaper that Rathdowne would not be a candidate, and Crofton was chosen and elected. The three elections had produced the three candidates Wellington wanted, and had avoided the candidacy of the one he did not want.

By this time peers of the reactionary hue of Roden and Rathdowne were beginning to be more trouble than they were worth, and Wellington was obviously willing to throw them over. But the duke had a new scheme. On 9 November Peel wrote that 'I think you are quite right about the Irish representative peerage, and that it will be better for *us* to do nothing in respect to the next vacancy.' On 6 December Wellington wrote to Peel: 'I entertain no doubt but that we have it in our power to carry the election for any candidate who may have reasonable pretensions, against any other. But it is best that the Irish resident peers should decide for themselves.' He continued later in the same letter: 'I am for making them feel that they have themselves an interest in these elections ... This is not easy and it is very troublesome, but it appears to me the only practical mode of proceeding'.[29] As a matter of fact, it was not all that difficult. During parliamentary sessions, all that was required was a meeting at Apsley House. When parliament was not sitting, it involved writing half a dozen letters to influential Irish peers. Wellington was left in the middle, a position which had served him well.

For the election of the 16 representative Scottish peers, the system of control became tighter than it had been under Liverpool. At the beginning of 1828, Lord Melville claimed: 'I really do not happen to know what steps Lord Liverpool used to take in regard to the election of Scottish peers – I mean as to intimating his wishes.'[30] What Melville meant was that he did not know how Liverpool got round word of whom he wanted elected: once the candidates were known no one could have accused Melville of not knowing how to elect them. But when in the 1832 election the conservatives decided to put forward their own candidates to challenge those of the government (unlike the Irish peers, the Scottish peers had to stand at every general election), tighter organization was necessary. Now Conservatives must stick together and vote only for the conservative candidates. This election was managed by a committee of three, Melville, the earl of Lauderdale and the duke of Buccleuch. They did very well; they put up 15 candidates and elected all 15.[31] Wellington was not so intimately involved in the election of Scottish as of Irish peers, but they were even more loyal. Still, though the Irish peers could sometimes be difficult, they generally supported the government, as it was in their interest to do; for even if once elected they were no longer reliant on government for their seats, as the Scottish peers were, governments could still do good things for their needy Irish dependents,

---

[28] Southampton U.L., WP2/63/17: Wellington to Peel, 24 Oct. 1839.

[29] Southampton U.L., WP2/63/87; /128.

[30] *Ibid.*, 917/16: Melville to Edward Drummond, n.d.

[31] H.M.C., *Wellington*, I, 31.

and after their deaths there were their successors to be thought of. Forty-four votes gave Wellington and leaders who followed him very considerable power.

Wellington did not persuade by great oratory. Indeed he told Lord Stanley in 1846 that before he succeeded Liverpool in the Lords in 1827, 'I had not I believe once spoke in Parliament for twenty years.'[32] That was an exaggeration but not much of one. He never developed into a great parliamentary speaker. He could give a good, clear speech, at some length, even on very complicated questions, as long as they were on subjects with which he felt comfortable, especially military and foreign affairs; but sometimes even on finances and taxation. Yet, at the same time, and especially when he felt compelled to take notice of remarks made before his, he could get hopelessly lost, or at any rate forget the real point of what he had got up to say. A great part of his speeches between his resignation in 1830 and the passage of the Reform Bill were spent in repetitious justifications of the policies of his government. At the same time, he could be very good in quick repartee. But he gave very few, if any, really great speeches. What he aimed at was making powerful interventions in debate, the shorter the better; as, for example, when at the end of the 1828 debate on Lord Eldon's amendment to add 'I am a Protestant' to the declaration required of all taking office after the repeal of the Test and Corporation Acts, he rose just before the vote and stated simply that though he was not ready for catholic emancipation, 'no man, on the other hand, is more determined that I am to give my vote against any proposition which, like the present, appears to have for its object a fresh enactment against Roman Catholics'.[33] He knew, and some others would have, that he was acting against the express wishes of the king. In any case, there was enough doubt about the status of Eldon's amendment to require clarification of the government's position. Wellington clarified it.

With his approach to leadership, Wellington was not very particular about whether he appeared to be in charge of a question or not. Often he opened debate on measures, but probably more often than most leaders he left it to others to do so. The Municipal Corporations Bill in 1835 was not the first important measure of which he put Lyndhurst in charge, and it was certainly not the last. Yet, whatever the appearances, behind the scenes Wellington remained in charge, swaying party meetings, organizing votes, and directing strategy. As Aberdeen testified of the duke's performance at the end of the 1840 session, he had 'never known such an instance of his power and influence'. In the following decade of conservative government it might have seemed as if his power, and powers, were declining. Yet, at the end, in 1846, deserted by his lieutenant and designated successor as well as by the conservative whip, virtually alone, Wellington's leadership of the Lords had never been more masterly.[34]

---

[32] Southampton U.L., WP2/138/41–4: draft Wellington to Stanley, n.d.

[33] R. W. Davis, 'Wellington and the "Open Question": The Issue of Catholic Emancipation, 1821–1829', *Albion*, XXIX (1997), 41.

[34] I. McLean, 'Wellington and the Corn Laws 1845–6: A Study in Heresthetic', in *Wellington Studies III*, ed. Woolgar, 227–56.

The Third Marquess of Lansdowne

JOHN POWELL

Henry Petty-Fitzmaurice, third marquess of Lansdowne (1780–1863),[1] was almost universally praised for his leadership in the house of lords between 1842 and his retirement in 1858. The assessment of Henry Brougham, not given to indiscriminate praise, is representative of most accounts from both sides of the House:

> His talents for business ... were very great; his powers of debating equally distinguished; and he showed the greatest of all qualities in rising with the occasion; for no man ever led any assembly more admirably in all respects – both of temper, judgment, readiness, resources in debate, and excellent speaking – than he did, when the place of leader devolved upon him in 1846.... He always was above the narrow-minded spirit of mere party and coterie. But nothing can be more pure and unsullied than his party honour at all times.[2]

Although Brougham's assessment was written shortly after Lansdowne's death, many in the same vein were written during his lifetime.[3] Even at the end of his career, he remained an influential whig, important in maintaining liberal governments, and an elder statesman, whose advice was sought by Queen Victoria.[4] It is not necessary to take Brougham at face value – there was considerable disagreement, for instance, over the quality of Lansdowne's speaking – in order to recognize that he was considered a figure of political weight during his lifetime, courted by Pitt, Fox, Grenville, Canning, Grey, Melbourne, Russell, Aberdeen and Palmerston. Such accounts, however, do not rest easily beside Jonathan Parry's recent assessment that no man 'served so long and left so little mark'.[5] Most historians, like Parry, have taken the glowing

---

[1] Lansdowne has no biography. See 'Marquess of Lansdown [*sic*]' in *Public Characters. Biographical and Characteristic Sketches* (2 vols, 1828), I, 85–96; 'The Marquess of Lansdowne' in *The British Cabinet in 1853* (1853), pp. 45–69; Harriet Martineau, *Biographical Sketches* (New York, [1869]), pp. 329–37; Abraham Hayward, *Selected Essays* (2 vols, 1878), II, 359–78. A vivid account of Lansdowne's domestic life, with a good deal on his political affairs between 1818 and 1844, can be found in *The Journal of Thomas Moore*, ed. Wilfred S. Dowden (6 vols, Newark, 1983–91).

[2] Henry Brougham, *The Life and Times of Henry Lord Brougham* (3 vols, Edinburgh, 1871), II, 490–1; also *George Douglas, Eighth Duke of Argyll, Autobiography and Memoirs, 1823–1900*, ed. the duchess of Argyll (2 vols, 1906), I, 375–6.

[3] See, for instance, Sydney Smith to J. A. Murray, 4 June 1843, in *The Letters of Sydney Smith*, ed. Nowell C. Smith (2 vols, Oxford, 1853), II, 784; Mary Hardcastle, *Life of John, Lord Campbell, Lord High Chancellor of Great Britain* (2 vols, 1881), II, 207–8.

[4] Bodleian Library, Hughenden MSS B/xx/5/123: Derby to Disraeli, 18 Dec. 1853; *Autobiography and Memoirs*, ed. Argyll, I, 363, 513. Naotaka Kimizuka, 'Elder Statesmen and British Party Politics: Wellington, Lansdowne and the Ministerial Crises in the 1850s', *Parliamentary History*, XVII (1998), 355–72; and *idem*, 'Ministers without Portfolio in Modern British Politics', *Shigaku-Zasshi*, CVII (1998), 65–88.

[5] Jonathan Parry, *The Rise and Fall of Liberal Government in Victorian Britain* (New Haven, 1993), p. 327.

descriptions of Lansdowne as mere obituary praise of a cultured, well-born peer who failed to distinguish himself in a major office of state. A careful examination of Lansdowne's leadership of the house of lords will suggest an unconventional path to the leadership, and the difficulty in using Lansdowne's experience as a guide to the development of the office generally.

Indeed, it is impossible to say exactly when Lansdowne 'led' in the Lords. He performed many of the functions of leader in his first year in the House (1809–1810), including speaking frequently on behalf of his party. As early as 1818 Tierney sought party support for Lansdowne's leadership following one of Grey's tentative retirements, though Grey thought it best not to formally choose a leader. By 1826 Grey privately acknowledged Lansdowne as 'the person best qualified to undertake the chief direction of the party'.[6] Lansdowne acted decidedly as party leader in the coalition building of 1826–28, though he disclaimed that he was doing so. Though leading the whigs when he joined the Canning ministry in 1827, the tory Lord Goderich actually led in the Lords. Under Grey (1830–34) and Melbourne (1834, 1835–41), he had no formal position of leadership, but due to the personalities of the prime ministers frequently spoke on behalf of the government and organized the moderate elements in the party. He was then almost universally acknowledged as whig leader in the Lords between 1842 and 1858, though Aberdeen, as Peelite prime minister, formally led the House from 1852 to 1855; and Grey, Clarendon and Granville handled many of the more laborious duties after 1850. Even in 1855 when Granville was chosen as successor, he assumed that it would be as 'temporary *locum tenens*', and that it would 'not be necessary to make any distinct statement to the House' as to leadership. When Lansdowne told Palmerston explicitly that he did not wish to lead the Lords, he nevertheless remained willing 'on some particular occasions to represent the government'.[7] The unusual appointment of Lansdowne as minister without portfolio (1852–58) suggested that he would retain some aspects of leadership in the upper House, and Granville himself did not imagine that he had fully assumed the position until 1858, when Lansdowne finally stopped attending the Lords.

Lansdowne has been called by David Large the 'first recognizable modern leader for the government in the Lords' (1846–1852), but no one has yet examined the nature of his leadership, or tried to explain why he was considered so successful by those who knew him, despite his frequent opposition to major legislative initiatives from the whig party leader, Lord John Russell. Large based his judgment upon three principal points. First, because Lansdowne did not serve as party leader as had Grey and Melbourne, he gave character to the position of leader in the Lords 'as a distinct institution'. Second, he carried 'the main burden of speaking' for the party in the upper House. Finally, he took 'steps to organize a following'.[8] In the absence of a formal election or an established office, these are useful standards for determining who

---

[6] Grey to Holland, 16 Feb. 1826, in Austin Mitchell, *The Whigs in Opposition* (Oxford, 1967), p. 28–32.

[7] Bodl. Lib., MS Clar dep Irish, 1A, box 7: Bessborough to Clarendon, 2 Apr. [1851]; Edmond Fitzmaurice, *The Life of Second Earl Granville, 1815–1891* (2 vols, 1905), I, 95–6, 294. Cf. E. A. Smith, *The House of Lords in British Politics and Society, 1815–1911* (1992), pp. 105–6.

[8] David Large, 'The Decline of "the Party of the Crown" and the Rise of Parties in the House of Lords, 1783–1837', *English Historical Review*, LXXVIII (1963), 694.

led the whigs in the house of lords. The process of becoming leader and exercising leadership there was, however, so complex that a simple application of these tests does not confirm that Lansdowne was the 'first recognizable modern leader'. The most fundamental issues remain largely unexamined. Who exactly was Lansdowne leading, and for whom did he speak? Considering that Lansdowne was, more than anyone else, responsible for forcing Russell to abandon reform bills in 1849, 1851, 1852 and 1853, and that he led successful assaults on major Irish initiatives, especially the income tax and permanent provision for outdoor relief, it is impossible to glibly state that he led the whigs and spoke for the party leader. Nor does the evidence suggest that he was 'guilty of a certain pedantry and archaism' in refraining from definitive use of the term 'leadership of the House of Lords'. Sainty argues that by late 1840s the 'the term came to be universally accepted as the description of the peer responsible for conducting the business of the government in the House of Lords', as if 'the business of the government' was all of a piece.[9] A careful examination of Lansdowne's leadership among the whigs will demonstrate that while he managed the whig party apparatus while in office, he consistently spoke on behalf of the large moderate element among the whigs, and for an anti-radical evolution of the party. And although he was an able lieutenant to Russell in the work of the government, the absence of a clear party programme enabled him to consistently defy important legislative initiatives without incurring the slightest imputation of disloyalty.

1

Henry Petty met the first requisite for whig leadership, that of being well-born. In addition to being one of the ten largest landowners in the realm, his father, Lord Shelburne, had been prime minister (1782–84). Petty studied under Dugald Stewart in Edinburgh, and there came into close association with a set of brilliant young men including Palmerston, Brougham, Francis Horner, Francis Jeffrey and Sydney Smith, the latter three founders of the *Edinburgh Review* (1802). If the doctrines of the Scottish enlightenment were not in general favour with the grand whigs, it was impossible for them to overlook Petty's control of three seats in the house of commons and his intimate connexions with the new mouthpiece of the whig party. After taking an M.A. from Trinity College, Cambridge, he toured the continent with Bentham's disciple and translator, Etienne Dumont, before entering political life in 1801 for the family borough of Calne. When Fox and Grenville formed their 'ministry of all the talents' following Pitt's death in 1806, the precocious Petty was made chancellor of the exchequer at 25 years of age. Although some doubt has been cast upon the quality of his performance in the office, he was one of the few whigs who understood or cared about the intricacies of political economy.[10] The death of Petty's brother on 15 November

---

[9] J. C. Sainty, 'The Origin of the Leadership of the House of Lords', *Bulletin of the Institute of Historical Research*, XLVII (1974), 66.

[10] Peter Jupp, *Lord Grenville, 1759–1834* (Oxford, 1985), pp. 373, 378, 395–8; cf. Denis Gray, *Spencer Perceval. The Evangelical Prime Minister, 1762–1812* (Manchester, 1963), pp. 353–5. On Lansdowne's understanding of finance, see B.L., Add. MS 51547: Holland to Grey, 2 Sept. 1825; 7 Nov. 1825; *Journal of Thomas Moore*, ed. Dowden, VI, 854; Brougham, *Life of Brougham*, II, 490.

The Third Marquess of Lansdowne, by Henry Walton
By courtesy of the National Portrait Gallery, London.

1809 further confused an already vexed situation.[11] Petty, having assumed his place in the Lords as the third marquess of Lansdowne, was sorely missed in the Commons, where he had shown energy and initiative, and was thrown into the upper House where Lord Grenville and Lord Grey already sat. Grenville and Grey together led the party between 1807 and 1817, but neither put much heart into organizing the opposition, and both renounced the leadership on more than one occasion.[12]

---

[11] Michael Roberts, *The Whig Party, 1807–1812* (2nd edn, New York, 1965), pp. 311–16, 319. The importance of Petty's succession was noted by Wellington in Spain.

[12] Grenville's appointment by Pitt as leader in the Lords in 1790 was 'a turning point in the evolution of the position', but there was no steady development of the position among whigs. According to Peter

Between 1809 and the formation of the Canning ministry in 1827, Lansdowne was the most consistently visible whig leader in the house of lords. His energy, versatility and readiness in debate kept him constantly in the forefront of whig politics. When the Grenville-Grey alliance broke down at the end of the 1817 session, and both strongly suggested the possibility of retirement, Lansdowne was immediately scouted as a possible leader, though he recognized that the party was too badly divided over foreign affairs, the suspension of habeas corpus, and questions of economy to be effectively led. The whigs were, he wrote, little more than a collection of 'persons' and 'small parties of persons opposed to, or unconnected with, the Administration', pursuing their own causes according to 'their own tastes and tempers'.[13] As a result of these divisions, he was already beginning to identify with the 'mass of political opinion', not quite devoted to party, which would form the basis of his future support.[14]

The death of George III offered prospects of a new administration, which also brought Grey out of the shadows. By 1820 Lansdowne had already determined that any new government 'could not be formed upon a narrow party basis', and there was persistent talk of Lansdowne as the lynchpin in a moderate tory-whig alliance, a position that kept him in the political foreground. By 1825, the catholic question offered ground for a possible coalition. Lansdowne, already acting the part of leader in the Lords, co-operated with Brougham to push the catholic question forward, despite opposition within the party.[15] With the death of the ultra-protestant duke of York and Liverpool's stroke, in 1827 the cause of catholic emancipation appeared to be at a crossroads. The stakes were high, both for the future of the party system in Britain and for peace in Ireland.[16] After complicated negotiations, beginning in late April Lansdowne, Tierney, Devonshire and Carlisle agreed to join Canning's new government, though Lansdowne refused to take office until the 1827 session had ended in order to avoid the appearance of compromising previous political commitments. Lansdowne declined the foreign office, considering appointment to the home office with its responsibility for Ireland a *sine qua non*. Though his commitment to catholic emancipation was questioned by some because he did not make it a condition of accepting office, he did secure appointment of the pro-catholic Melbourne (then William Lamb) as Irish secretary, as well as his own appointment as home secretary.

---

[12] (*continued*) Jupp, for instance, 'Grenville was the acknowledged leader of the main body of politicians opposed to the Portland, Perceval, and Liverpool administrations', but this 'did not mean that he was necessarily regarded, or had been specifically chosen, as the best person to direct the day to day affairs of the Opposition'. Sainty, 'Origins of the Leadership', pp. 62–3; E. A. Smith, *Lord Grey, 1764–1845* (Oxford, 1990), pp. 205–6; Jupp, *Lord Grenville*, p. 413.

[13] Henry E. Huntington Library, STG 78 (25): Grenville to Buckingham, 13 May 1817; Ellis Archer Wasson, *Whig Renaissance. Lord Althorp and the Whig party, 1782–1845* (New York, 1987), p. 129; Lansdowne to Brougham, 28 July 1817, in Brougham, *Life of Brougham*, II, 318–19.

[14] Cited in Chester W. New, *The Life of Henry Brougham to 1830* (Oxford, 1961), p. 180.

[15] *The Journal of Henry Edward Fox*, ed. the earl of Ilchester (1923), p. 155; *The Private Letters of Princess Lieven to Prince Metternich, 1820–1826*, ed. Peter Quennell (New York, 1938), pp. 317–18, 337, 362, 366–7; Huntington Lib., STG 89 (47): Charles Wynn to Buckingham, 9 Sept. 1821; STG 92 (10): Wynn to Buckingham, 26 Feb. 1825.

[16] Thomas Spring-Rice to E. J. Littleton, 8 Mar. 1827, in *The Formation of Canning's Ministry, February to August 1827*, ed. Arthur Aspinall (Camden 3rd ser., LIX, 1937), pp. 76–7, 81, p. 34; Oliver MacDonagh, *Daniel O'Connell. The Hereditary Bondsman, 1775–1829* (1988), p. 233.

If the total number of whig places in the Canning government was small (three of 15 in the cabinet, nine of 52 overall), it was widely believed that Lansdowne was well positioned to exert greater influence with Canning in the future. With Canning's poor health, the good will of the king, and the backing of 'powerful and active adherents', for a brief time it appeared that Lansdowne might eventually succeed as prime minister. The prospect presented, in Sir Francis Burdett's words, 'a career open to honourable ambition' which had 'seldom offered itself to any man'.[17]

The achievements of the Canning coalition never matched its promise, and the possibilities afforded Lansdowne as the principal coalitionist among the whigs soon exposed both his personal weaknesses and the weakness of the whigs as a party.[18] Grey, who hated Canning and disapproved of the coalition, remained aloof, and served as a rallying point for Ellenborough, Jersey, Bedford, Rosslyn, Albemarle and others reluctant to make common cause with Canning. Althorp, Ebrington and Lord John Russell were 'reluctant to leave their old opposition places'.[19] Even supporters believed that Lansdowne had not been forceful enough in asserting either their claims to office, or a promise of his own claim to the leadership of the house of lords in the next session. Goderich's succession as prime minister, following Canning's death on 8 August 1827, further complicated Lansdowne's claim to leadership in the upper House. The perception of weakness was reinforced when Lansdowne was persuaded by the king not to resign following the appointment of the anti-catholic J. C. Herries to the exchequer. Lansdowne admitted that 'another concession would ruin us completely'.[20] There were plausible reasons for staying on. It was a measure of satisfaction to some that the change of ministry involved no approach to the tories. In order to maintain the government intact as far as possible, however, Lansdowne found it necessary to agree that no additional places would be given to whigs, including Holland. 'I hear', wrote Fremantle to the duke of Buckingham on 16 September, that 'Lord Lansdowne is content with all that was done by Lord Goderich.'[21] Whether or not this exaggerates the actual case, Lansdowne appeared to followers of Grey and Russell to be too eager to please as the Goderich ministry limped on to its January demise.

Patience and circumstance, if not indecision, might have cost Lansdowne the leadership of the Lords, possibly the succession to Canning (though this was unlikely), and, at least for a time, his reputation as a government broker. Lansdowne, it seemed, lacked the instinct of a great leader. When pressed to exercise 'a little vigorous mischief', 'bringing matters to a crisis by some decisive step that would enable him to break from his false position with éclat', he responded with the characteristic

---

[17] Burdett to Lansdowne, 27 Apr. 1827; Arbuthnot to Peel, 6 July 1827; Bathhurst to Arbuthnot, 17 July 1827, in *Formation of Canning's Ministry*, ed. Aspinall, pp. 192, 253, 264. On Lansdowne's backing, see Smith, *Lord Grey*, p. 243; J. T. Ward, *Sir James Graham* (1967), pp. 75, 146–7; Mitchell, *Whigs in Opposition*, pp. 198–201.

[18] This combination of personal and party weakness is illuminated in Joe Bord, 'Patronage, the Lansdowne Whigs and the Problem of the Liberal Centre, 1827–8', *English Historical Review*, CXVII (2002), 78–93.

[19] Mitchell, *Whigs in Opposition*, pp. 200–1.

[20] Cited in *ibid.*, pp. 204–5; Croker memorandum, 11 Aug. 1827, in *The Croker Papers, 1808–1857*, ed. Bernard Pool, (New York, 1967), p. 107.

[21] *Memoirs of the Court of George IV, 1820–1830*, ed. the duke of Buckingham and Chandos, (2 vols, 1859), II, 349–50.

self-effacement that kept him from the highest positions of leadership – 'Yes – that's all very well – but I must take care and not do mischief to the cause I have at heart in consulting my own éclat or convenience.'[22] Though his personal position stood very high in early 1827, the whigs were too weak to insist on catholic emancipation. The choice was either loyalty to Canning or a return to divided opposition. Lansdowne had tried and failed to reorganize the whigs in Grey's absence. But political insiders on both sides knew the difficulties he faced, and most attributed the failure as much to political complexities as to personal failure.

Lansdowne's reputation was harmed, but hardly destroyed, by the manoeuvres of 1827–28. Following the demise of the Canning coalition, whigs frequently spoke in private of his deficiencies. The duke of Bedford considered Lansdowne a 'dupe,' and Lord John Russell believed him 'too yielding, too mild'. Holland thought of Lansdowne and his followers as 'feeble men'; the young whigs believed him unfit for service, and Creevey positively ridiculed his weakness. By the fall of Grey's ministry in 1834, Lansdowne had become, according to Howick (later third Earl Grey), a 'mere cypher', and Althorp hoped he would go.[23] Such private comments, as widespread as they may seem, are not good indicators of Lansdowne's position in the party. Some reflected personal pique; some were naturally born of the disappointment with the coalition experiment; some suggested genuine weaknesses. In the end, however, the people who made the governments – Grey, Melbourne and Russell – all believed that Lansdowne was indispensable. He still had the support of moderate whigs, both O'Connell and the king looked favorably on his conduct, and the tories continued to worry about his 'future opposition'.[24] In 1828 he once again threw himself into the effort for catholic emancipation. In December, he wrote to leading whigs, urging that they 'buckle on' their 'armour at the very outset of the approaching session and fight the catholic question resolutely as a party'. It is telling that in trying to rouse the whigs, Lansdowne eschewed any modern notion of party-building, feeling that it would be neither advisable nor necessary to 'effect a strict party alliance between all the scattered fragments who are friendly to our principle'. Instead, he simply wished for agreement on the catholic question, after which it was understood that 'all were individually at liberty'.[25] This smallest of concessions to party discipline, applied to a principle upon which almost all agreed, still failed to draw the party together. Lansdowne nevertheless was viewed as leader of the whigs in the house of lords.[26] With his pocket borough of Calne returning two members, he still had the

---

[22] *Journal of Thomas Moore*, ed. Dowden, III, 1125.

[23] Spencer Walpole, *The Life of Lord John Russell* (2 vols, 1889), I, 135, 137; Wasson, *Whig Renaissance*, pp. 152–6, 187, 318; *The Creevey Papers*, ed. Sir Herbert Maxwell (2 vols, 1904) II, 128, 154; *The Holland House Diaries, 1831–1840*, ed. Abraham Kriegel (1977), pp. 108–9; Richard Brent, *Liberal Anglican Politics. Whiggery Religion, and Reform 1830–1841* (Oxford, 1987), pp. 110–11.

[24] MacDonagh, *O'Connell. The Hereditary Bondsman*, p. 248; Grey to Creevey, 13 Dec. 1827, in *The Creevey Papers*, II, 139–40; Lyndhurst to Knighton, 11 Jan. 1828, in *The Letters of King George IV, 1812–1830*, ed. Arthur Aspinall (3 vols, Cambridge, 1938), III, 362–3.

[25] Mitchell, *The Whigs in Opposition*, pp. 211–14.

[26] See, for instance, John Roebuck, *History of the Whig Ministry of 1830* (1852), p. 144. This recognition is that of an outsider observing the outward functions of leader, particularly with regard to speaking on behalf of government measures. Roebuck otherwise pays little attention to Lansdowne.

independent power to bring forward powerful protégés.[27] Lansdowne too was patron to a variety of influential moderate politicians and publicists who looked to him for political guidance, the group that Peter Mandler has referred to as the 'Bowood set'.[28]

While Grey was unquestionably recognized as leader after his return in November 1830, he considered Lansdowne's support essential, both in terms of practical support and influence with moderates. Though Lansdowne declined any major cabinet post, the prime minister gave him the position he wanted – lord president of the council; appointed his nominee – Palmerston – to the foreign office; and made Lansdowne part of the inner group of advisors.[29] In return, he got a ready spokesman in the Lords to help with the multitude of pressing issues and a strong supporter of the government's Irish policy.[30] It was both symbolically and practically important that Lansdowne, foremost in his desire 'to preserve our settled institutions', made the first ministerial declaration of the new government as 'a friend to amendment in the representative system'.[31] In terms of reform policy, Lansdowne was a useful counterweight to the more advanced whigs. Though committed to political reform, Grey was not anxious to go so far as Russell, Brougham, Althorp and the Radical wing.[32] Lansdowne played a small but active role in shaping the cabinet debate, vigorously opposing the secret ballot and a new creation of peers except as a last resort, but supporting the necessity of the principle of reform. Unwavering commitment to law enforcement and anti-radicalism reassured tory waverers on both reform and Irish policy. On foreign policy issues, Lansdowne provided an important connexion to the Canningites, especially Palmerston, and he was intimately acquainted with many of the most important figures in French politics and diplomacy. In his political moderation on most issues, his influence was especially strong with Spring Rice, Auckland and Clarendon. As urbane and co-operative as Lansdowne was, there were limits to his reforming spirit, and many moderates tended to look to him, not so much as a formal leader, but as a wise judge of just how far an independent and 'reasonable' reformer should go.[33]

Despite Grey's careful management of the cabinet, deep divisions over Irish policy remained. By May 1834, Stanley, Graham, Ripon and Richmond had resigned, and

---

[27] Brougham to Grey, 17 Feb. 1830, in Brougham, *Life of Brougham*, III, 29–30; Macaulay to Lansdowne, 5 Dec. 1833, in G. O. Trevelyan, *Life and Letters of Lord Macaulay* (new edn, 1888), p. 250.

[28] Peter Mandler, *Aristocratic Government in the Age of Reform. Whigs and Liberals, 1830–1852* (Oxford, 1990), pp. 96–104.

[29] Durham Univ. Lib., Grey Papers: Lansdowne to Grey, 18 Nov. 1830; B.L., Add. MS 51555: Grey to Holland, 18 Nov. 1830; Smith, *Lord Grey*, p. 280; Sir Denis Le Marchant, *Memoir of John Charles, Viscount Althorp, third Earl Spencer* (1876), pp. 259, 263.

[30] On the close cooperation of Stanley and Lansdowne in Irish policy, see Hawkins, 'Lord Derby', in *Lords of Parliament. Studies 1714–1914*, ed. R. W. Davis, (Sanford, CA, 1995), pp. 137–8; Hansard, *Parl. Debs*, 3rd ser., X, 1269–70, 8 Mar. 1832; XVI, 821–2, 19 Mar. 1833; *Holland House Diaries*, ed. Kriegel, p. 149; A. D. Kriegel, 'The Irish Policy of Lord Grey's Government', *English Historical Review*, LXXXVI (1971), 22–45.

[31] Hansard, *Parl. Debs*, 3rd ser., I, 604–5, 22 Nov. 1830.

[32] Le Marchant, *Memoir of Earl Spencer*, pp. 402–3; J. R. M. Butler, *The Passing of the Great Reform Bill* (1964), p. 184; *Holland House Diaries*, ed. Kriegel, pp. 167, 169; Michael Brock, *The Great Reform Act* (Aldershot, 1993), pp. 163–4, 202, 236.

[33] Ward, *Sir James Graham*, pp. 146–47; B.L., Lansdowne Papers (3) 32, no. 102: Clarendon to Lansdowne, 14 Dec. 1851.

Lansdowne, fully as conservative on the Irish church, was on the verge of doing likewise. Hawkins observes that Stanley's resignation marked the failure of Grey's strategy of 'using Stanley as a counterbalance to the extreme reformers within the government'.[34] With Grey himself only a few months from leaving office, it is easy to see the May resignations as the effective end of his ministry. Grey did, however, have a final card to play in checking Russell and radicalism in the party. By threatening to resign himself, he kept Lansdowne in the cabinet, and with him the broad base of moderate whiggery. As a part of the negotiation, Lansdowne successfully lobbied for the promotion of Auckland and Spring Rice to the cabinet, 'good appointments in the 'Conservative (not Tory) line', according to Palmerston. Though Brougham's view that this created a 'Lansdowne House Cabinet' was exaggerated, Grey believed that Lansdowne's support was necessary for maintaining the ministry into the summer, in the face of both the tories and the advanced reformers among the whigs themselves.[35] This was an important moment for both Lansdowne and the whig party. Grey's confidence in Lansdowne's ability to maintain the moderate wing of the whig party against radical encroachments indicated to those who had doubted Lansdowne since 1828 that he was still a political factor.

Although Lansdowne held no new position of leadership in Melbourne's ministry (1835–1841), several factors enabled him to exert more influence in the Lords than would be customary with a prime minister in the same House. Lansdowne, for instance, was one of the few able debaters who routinely defended the government. According to Holland, Lansdowne alone came to the prime minister's aid, 'as in truth we ought'.[36] Second, Melbourne's diffidence toward most aspects of governance provided ministers considerable latitude in the exercise of their powers. Ministers handled their own departmental business as energetically as they pleased, while the organizing work of the party – making of lists, management of proxies, whipping-in – was slackly attended to or sometimes left completely undone. This slackness generally heightened the value of the work that Lansdowne did informally on behalf of the government.[37] Finally, Lansdowne's influence in the party increased under Melbourne because he was working primarily on behalf of the moderate cause. His goals were essentially anti-radical, and he could therefore count on the support of the tory opposition to advanced measures.[38] In 1840, for instance, Lansdowne and Lyndhurst co-operated in an intricate procedural negotiation in order to pass

[34] Hawkins, 'Lord Derby', pp. 145–6.

[35] Palmerston and Brougham cited in Mandler, *Aristocratic Government*, pp. 153–4. There is some question over Lansdowne's initiative in Auckland's promotion, but the effect of promoting Lansdowne's protégé was the same in any event. See Brougham, *Life of Brougham*, III, 250; *Holland House Diaries*, ed. Kriegel, p. 254; *Three Early Nineteenth Century Diaries*, ed. A. Aspinall (1952), pp. 380–1; Wasson, *Whig Renaissance*, pp. 308–10.

[36] Cited in Fraser, *House of Lords*, II, 847; *Lord Melbourne's Papers*, ed. Lloyd C. Sanders (1889), pp. 380–3.

[37] See in particular discussion of management of the Irish Municipal Corporations Bill (1839), Robert S. Fraser, 'The House of Lords in the First Parliament of Queen Victoria, 1837–41', Cornell University Ph.D., 1967, pp. 212–14, 503–7; Walpole, *Life of Russell*, I, 326–7.

[38] An excellent discussion of the political position which Lansdowne held, believing that 'real differences of opinion should not altogether coincide with party divisions', is found in Donald Southgate, *The Passing of the Whigs*, 1832–1886 (1962), pp. 65–7.

the Irish Municipal Corporations Bill. Though both radicals and ultra-tories were dissatisfied, the five-year struggle demonstrated that incremental change was possible when extreme measures were avoided.[39]

Following Melbourne's stroke in 1842, Russell and Lansdowne were the obvious leaders in the Commons and Lords, respectively. There was still no formal process for choosing the leader in the upper House, however, and Lansdowne chose not to risk the presumption of formally assuming the title. With Melbourne still keen to give advice, and the party sensitive to the former prime minister's delicate state, Lansdowne took up the task of leadership while avoiding its trappings.[40] Lord Campbell recalled, as a newly created peer, that Lansdowne was 'naturally to be looked up to, but, out of delicacy, he both ostensibly and privately declined to act as our leader in the Lords'. Because 'he would not even give the usual eve-of-session dinner', Campbell was 'left to the freedom of my own will'.[41] Thus, although Lansdowne was the obvious leader, in 1842 it appeared that historic sensibilities would doom the whigs, once more, to being led from the rear.

The case of Lansdowne leading the Lords in the 1840s was a near perfect fit of man and circumstance. The country had taken a cautious step toward reform, but was not eager for more; the Commons was the dominant House, but the Lords still played a prominent political role; the landed aristocracy no longer monopolized wealth and status, but they retained enormous social prestige. In each of these areas, Lansdowne had accommodated himself to change, but was prepared to openly defend what remained of British traditions and the mixed constitution. Lansdowne's political weight as a patron of moderates was multiplied in a fractured political system where party loyalties had been discounted and reform was considered less important than stability. It was further multiplied in the face of Irish famine, continental revolution, and perpetual instability in France. Clarendon spoke for moderates generally when he wrote to Lansdowne from Ireland in the midst of negotiations over Russell's Reform Bill of 1851: 'if you concurred ... I should expect the Bill to meet with support from reasonable men and if you felt compelled to wash your hands of it the Govt. could not go on'.[42] If disaffected or excluded from a whig or coalition government – a course never seriously considered by Russell, Palmerston or Aberdeen – Lansdowne would have loomed as a dignified and experienced figure around whom moderate whigs and liberal tories might coalesce in combating the succession of crises that faced Russell's government. Lansdowne did not plan to undermine Russell, but he was unwilling to allow the prime minister to force radical measures on the cabinet.

---

[39] Southgate, *Passing of the Whigs*, p. 65; Fraser, 'House of Lords', pp. 687–90.

[40] Although there was little possibility of Melbourne's return to politics, he was still consulted, and within months of his death in November 1848, odd political roles were still being found for him to play. B.L., LP (3) 43: Russell to Lansdowne [15 Mar. 1848]; *Lord Melbourne's Papers*, ed. Sanders, pp. 512–28; L. G. Mitchell, *Lord Melbourne, 1779–1848* (Oxford, 1997), pp. 263–4; B.L., LP (3) 42, no. 14: Palmerston to Lansdowne, 4 Nov. 1842.

[41] Hardcastle, *Life of Campbell*, II, 173.

[42] B.L., LP (3) 32, no. 102: Clarendon to Lansdowne, 14 Dec. 1851.

2

Lansdowne brought an unusually full array of experience, skill and influence to the task of leading the whigs in the house of lords. Though never in the very first rank of debaters, he was capable of delivering effective and occasionally powerful speeches.[43] He was well educated, well read, experienced, and, best of all from the perspective of a short-handed party, ready and willing to speak on short notice. His habits of management were old-fashioned, relying on informal correspondence and conclaves, though he worked in fairly close co-ordination with the whips, Lords Strafford (1842–1850) and Bessborough (1850–1880), in summoning peers and watching attendance. Whipping in and management of proxies and lists were left largely to the whips themselves, except in 'real party fights'.[44] Clarendon seems to have assisted Lansdowne in organizing the peers, at least as early as 1845, though this was probably an informal arrangement based upon Lansdowne's health and workload.[45] Lansdowne, rather than the whips, was chiefly responsible for securing movers and seconders of the address, though this difficult duty was shared with Russell and the whips.[46] Principally utilizing traditional methods of private correspondence, rather than circulars or party meetings, Lansdowne prepared his colleagues for debate, and arranged speakers when sickness or other duties kept ministers or key advisers away from the House. When party conclaves were necessary, the party often repaired to Lansdowne House.

Lansdowne's combination of competence and experience is well illustrated in his handling of the sickness and eventual retirement of Lord Cottenham, which left the whigs without a lord chancellor in the House between March and July 1850, facing the 'unparalleled' difficulty of 'having no lawyer in the H. of Lords'. Having already spoken on some 40 separate issues during the session, including major debates on Ireland, the ecclesiastical commission, and the Don Pacifico affair, Lansdowne then became responsible for speaking on legal questions before the Lords. In contesting the bishop of London's attempt to extend the influence of ecclesiastical courts, on 3 June Lansdowne apologized for the absence of Cottenham, who, he observed, 'would have stated the objections ... with much greater authority and ability'. He then went on to powerfully and successfully oppose the second reading of the bill, with a knowledge of the history and precedent of the relationship between the privy council and ecclesiastical courts that could not have been matched by any other

---

[43] B.L., LP (3) 4: Broughton to Lansdowne, 9 June 1843.

[44] See Paul Hogan, 'Party Management in the House of Lords, 1846–1865', *Parliamentary History*, X (1991), 132; B.L., LP (3) 38, no. 115: Monteagle to Lansdowne [n.d.]; P.R.O., 30/22/8A, f. 46: Lansdowne to Russell, [30 July 1849]. It is clear, however, that Lansdowne remained in charge of proxy use. Bodl. Lib., Clar. Dep. Irish, 1A/7: Bessborough to Clarendon, 31 Dec. [?1850].

[45] In 1845 Clarendon sent invitations to the peers dinner prior to the address. B.L., LP (3) 38: Monteagle to Lansdowne, 25 Jan. 1845.

[46] Cf. Hogan, 'Party Management in the House of Lords', p. 137. Among much correspondence, see B.L., LP, (3) 43: Russell to Lansdowne, 10 Nov. 1847; B.L., LP, (3) 29: Wodehouse to Lansdowne, 10 Jan. 1851; P.R.O., 30/22/9J(2), f. 116: Lansdowne to Russell, 23 Dec. 1851; Bodl. Lib., Clar. Dep. Irish, 1A, Box 7: Bessborough to Clarendon, 29 Jan. [1851].

whig. When it became clear that Cottenham would be unable to return, Lansdowne arranged for Campbell, who had just been made chief justice of the queen's bench, to 'take charge' of judicial bills.[47]

The ability to energize supporters in the upper House was an important task for the leader in any party, but was especially difficult for the whigs, who stood in a permanent minority and who were historically less conditioned than the tories to follow party discipline. As Lansdowne reported to Russell on the Encumbered Estates Bill in July 1849, it was typically only through 'a mixture of threatening and coaxing' that bills and their necessary amendments could be passed.[48] Encouraging peers to be politically active meant more than simply seeing that they came to the House or sent a proxy for an important vote. In the Lords where the Peelites held the balance of power after 1846, successful legislating was usually about management in committee, where modifications leading to bipartisan support were hammered out. As Stanley wrote in May 1847, he was willing to accept rejection of amendments to the Irish Poor Relief Bill because the 'clause limiting the taxation was introduced pro forma in the Committee', but was unwilling to countenance a reversal of committee decisions.[49] Lansdowne assiduously organized committees, sought out experts, and kept cabinet ministers informed of their work, particularly when close divisions were impending.[50] By 1847, the burden of leadership was becoming exceedingly heavy, and there were few young men of obvious talent who might be expected to lend significant help. Clarendon could not think of a single whig in the Lords who might ease the burden on Lansdowne and Grey. With Lansdowne's gout worsening, by 1850 Grey and Clarendon had begun to perform many of the routine tasks of leadership in the Lords.

The sheer numerical weakness of active whigs made Lansdowne's appeal to moderates of great significance. Where Russell tended to be aloof, and actually to alienate supporters by his neglect, Lansdowne's personal kindness and political moderation encouraged potential supporters to identify themselves as whigs, and thus to bring their talents of debate and administration to the party. Lansdowne was instrumental in Granville's rapid promotion, and in the adherence of the duke of Argyll (b. 1823) and Baron Wodehouse (b. 1826), both from tory families. Argyll recalled his early experience when he wrote to Russell on the reform bill in 1853, hoping to avert Lansdowne's secession. Not only did he carry weight with the old whigs, but 'with the more moderate and liberal Conservatives' as well. 'I feel sure that if I were an independent member of the House at this moment, Lord

---

[47] Durham Univ. Lib., GRE/B113/4B/40: Lansdowne to Grey, [April 1850]; Hansard, *Parl. Debs*, 3rd ser., CXI, 620–8, 3 June 1850; Hardcastle, *Life of Campbell*, II, 253; B.L., LP (3), 32, no. 80: Clarendon to Lansdowne, 23 June 1850.

[48] P.R.O., 30/22/8A, f. 46: Lansdowne to Russell, [30 July 1848]; Peter Gray, *Famine, Land and Politics. British Government and Irish Society, 1843–1850* (Dublin, 1999), pp. 218–19. See too B.L., LP, (3) 31, no. 32: Clarendon to Lansdowne, 26 July 1848.

[49] B.L., LP, (3) 7: Derby to Lansdowne, 11 May 1847.

[50] Durham Univ. Lib., GRE/B113/4B/30: Lansdowne to Grey, July [1847]; B.L., LP (3) 43: Lansdowne to Russell [1847]; P.R.O., 30/22/7A, f. 94: Lansdowne to Russell, 14 Jan. 1848; P.R.O., 30/22/8A, ff. 46–47: Lansdowne to Russell, [30 July 1849]; Raikes Currie to Bertram Currie, 26 Sept. 1850, in B. W. Currie, *Recollections, Letters and Journals*, ed. C. L. Currie (2 vols, Roehampton 1901), I, 424–25; *The Correspondence of Lord Overstone*, ed. D. P. O'Brien, (3 vols, Cambridge, 1971), II, 321–2.

Lansdowne's opposition would go very far to awaken my alarm.'[51] The support of moderates, whatever their nominal political allegiance, might also lead to direct electoral advantage. In 1852, for instance, as A. W. Kinglake prepared for an 'arduous' (and unsuccessful) bid for parliament, he requested that he be allowed to bring his old Etonian friend, the tory Lovell Sealy, for a visit. 'I feel sure', Kinglake wrote, 'that I should gratify him very much if your kindness enabled me to offer him the privilege of passing an hour at Lansdowne House.'[52] Wodehouse's adherence to the whigs led directly to the election of liberals to two seats long held by tories in Norfolk.[53]

Maintaining the support of the old whigs, independent and idiosyncratic, was no small task, and no one was better equipped than Lansdowne for doing it. Well known for his equable temper and lack of dogmatism, he was adept at coddling difficult but influential whigs. This was important for securing votes, but even more valuable in encouraging a friendly attitude toward the party generally, and thus in limiting the flow of hostile motions, amendments, and behind-the-scenes cabals aimed at legislation or ministerial activity. The most troublesome of the independents – Brougham, Grey, and Monteagle (formerly Spring Rice) – were friends or long-time associates, and it was frequently recommended that Lansdowne include them in the work of the Lords – in part for their expertise, but also to keep them from firing vollies 'into the Whig flank' in debate.[54] Grey, though important to Russell's government, was a 'refractory ally'. From the breakdown of negotiations to form a ministry in 1845, he was a difficult colleague, and continued to be suspected of undermining Russell. Lansdowne's patience, however, helped keep him in the government, where his skills were badly needed. Grey became more temperate, and by 1850 emerged as an effective leader during Lansdowne's absences.[55] Monteagle was less personally abrasive, but by 1847 was mistrusted by many moderate whigs, especially Irish landlords, who believed that he was bringing to shame their honest attempts to grapple with the Irish dilemma by trying to enjoy all the advantages provided to landlords in the Poor Law Amendment Bill, while undermining the clauses which imposed burdens on them. Although Lansdowne was not enthusiastic about the measure, he recognized the importance of extending relief on the principle of 'equalising the burdens on the landlord and on the tenant', and finally prevailed in passing the measure by accepting a number of Stanley's more moderate amendments.[56] Brougham was a perpetual source of trouble, gifted in debate, but querulous and unconcerned with the fate

---

[51] *Autobiography and Memoirs*, ed. Argyll, I, 362–3; Argyll to Russell, 18 Dec. 1853, in *The Later Correspondence of Lord John Russell 1840–1878*, ed. G. P. Gooch (2 vols, 1925), II, 128.

[52] B.L., LP (3) 16: Kinglake to Lansdowne, 4 May 1852. On the importance of Lansdowne House, *see* Hardcastle, *Life of Campbell*, II, 207.

[53] P.R.O., 30/22/7A, f. 19: Boileau to Russell, 2 Jan. 1848; D. C. Moore, *The Politics of Deference. A Study in the Mid-Nineteenth Century English Political System* (Hassocks, 1979), pp. 295–7; *The Poll for . . . the Eastern Division of the County of Norfolk* (Norwich, 1858), p. ix; Norfolk and Norwich R.O., Kimberley Papers 3/1: Wodehouse to Raikes Currie, 11 Apr. 1857.

[54] B.L., Add. MS 47228, ff. 103–4: Lansdowne to Hobhouse, [20 Oct. 1844]; B.L., LP, (3) 31, nos. 52, 53: Clarendon to Lansdowne, 14, 27 Jan. 1849.

[55] F. A. Dreyer, 'The Whigs and the Political Crisis of 1845', *English Historical Review* LXXX (1965), 522–5, 529; P.R.O., 30/22/7C, ff. 97–100: Lansdowne to Russell [May 1848]; Bodl. Lib., Clar. Dep. Irish 1A/7: Bessborough to Clarendon, 4 Feb., 2 Apr. [1851].

[56] Hansard, *Parl. Debs*, 3rd ser., XCII, 569, 10 May 1847; Gray, *Famine, Land and Politics*, pp. 280–3.

of the whigs. As Lansdowne fended off the attempt by the bishop of London to extend the influence of ecclesiastical courts in 1850, for instance, Brougham criticized both Blomfield and Lansdowne, arguing with some pride that he found himself in a 'position not unusual with Members who belonged to no party in the State'.[57] While it was impossible to control Brougham, he might be flattered by seeking his advice, and bringing him into confidence before the session, when possible, in order to forestall rash interventions at the time of the queen's speech.[58]

Lansdowne was incomparable in mediating an infinite number of disputes involving many men of distinction both in and out of government, and the length of Russell's government – five years and eight months – owes as much to this as anything else. In the early years of opposition, Melbourne still brooded over his inactivity; Brougham stood ever ready to attack anyone; Palmerston violently disliked Clarendon and Ellice, Grey was impossibly vain and sensitive; Russell was cold and aloof; and Palmerston's presumption of authority offended generally.[59] With Russell so thin-skinned, Lansdowne assumed the role of party mediator, which otherwise might have fallen to the prime minister, and as a result further increased his influence within the party. Some issues were small but potentially destructive because of their personal nature. In 1844, for instance, Brougham wrote to Lansdowne, as a 'friend of Monteagle's', to complain that Monteagle's inattention to his duties had in effect made his position as comptroller-general of the receipt and issue at the exchequer a sinecure. Though Monteagle could never quite shake his indignation at Brougham's accusation, Lansdowne managed to smooth things over.[60] At other times, personal acrimony and mistrust threatened to bring down the government, especially when it involved Palmerston, who had no personal following but was enormously popular with the public.

Nothing better illustrates the ambiguities surrounding the responsibilities of the leader in the Lords than Lansdowne's position in relation to Russell and Palmerston, each of whom had a pronounced tendency to act without consultation.[61] Russell, for instance, had kept his closest political allies in the dark before publicly declaring for complete free trade in 1845, a position that could not command a majority in either house of parliament at the time. Lansdowne, though preferring a gradual reduction of duties, worked with Russell to investigate a possible conjunction with Peel. He and others in the party were nevertheless nonplussed at Russell's secrecy, and privately condemned him for taking 'a step so important as abandoning the course he had been pursuing in common with them'.[62] When Russell took the cabinet by surprise on 9 October 1849 with the announcement of his intention to bring forward in

---

[57] Hansard, *Parl. Debs*, 3rd ser., CXI, 628, 3 June 1850.

[58] Dreyer, 'The Whigs and the Political Crisis of 1845', pp. 525, 529; P.R.O., 30/22/7C, ff. 97–100; B.L., LP, (3) 31, no. 53: Clarendon to Lansdowne, 27 Jan. 1849; B.L., LP (3) 32, no. 86: Clarendon to Lansdowne, 7 Jan. 1851.

[59] 13 Aug. 1846, *The Greville Memoirs*, ed. Henry Reeve (8 vols, 1888), V, 337–9.

[60] B.L., LP (3), 38, nos. 71, 79, 79B: Monteagle to Lansdowne, 15, 17 Jan. 1844, Brougham to Lansdowne, 12 Jan. [1844].

[61] According to Charles Greville, it was Russell's 'custom' to act without consultation. *Greville Memoirs*, ed. Reeve, V, 304–305.

[62] B.L., LP (3), 31, no. 10: Clarendon to Lansdowne, 2 Dec. 1845; Dreyer, 'The Whigs and the Political Crisis of 1845', pp. 514–21.

the next session a measure for extending the franchise, Lansdowne and Palmerston reluctantly accepted that 'some extension of the right of voting might properly be made', but within weeks Russell was forced to abandon the measure.[63] Russell's customary secrecy was made worse by the succession of crises that often led to makeshift policies and more surprises. The Rate in Aid Bill, for instance, over which Lansdowne threatened to resign in February 1849, was the last alternative left to the government for providing urgent food aid to Ireland. Under the circumstances, it was not clear to Lansdowne and others exactly where party loyalty ended and blind subservience began.

Palmerston was just as inconsiderate of the corporate nature of the government. Although he routinely circulated dispatches to Lansdowne, he rarely sent copies of his private instructions. On several occasions Lansdowne, as leader of the Lords, was required to mediate or provide public cover for what were widely perceived as indiscretions on Palmerston's part, including his public execration of the Webster-Ashburton Treaty in 1842, the offer of 'advice' to the Spanish government in 1848, the release of guns to Sicily in 1849, and the Don Pacifico affair in 1850. Russell as prime minister was particularly sensitive to Palmerston's independence of action. Of the Spanish affair, he wrote to Lansdowne that Palmerston's dispatch was sent to Madrid 'two days before I saw it, and against the opinion I had expressed' to him. 'I must beg you to interfere before I say all I think.' After conferring with Palmerston in order to lay papers before the House, Lansdowne ably defended the 'character' of the government in embarrassing circumstances, leading Stanley to withdraw his hostile motion. As a result Palmerston agreed – at least for a time – that all future dispatches of importance would first be submitted to the prime minister.[64] It may be argued that Palmerston was scarcely brought into line with Russell's leadership, but he was kept in the government until December 1851, in substantial measure, because of Lansdowne's interventions. It was Lansdowne, too, who convinced Palmerston to join the Aberdeen coalition a year later.[65] At the same time that Lansdowne was protecting the integrity of the government, however, he was also aiding one of his strongest allies in resisting Russell's proposals for political and Irish land reform, and it was to Lansdowne that Palmerston looked as a potential centrist premier in the fall of 1852.[66] And while Lansdowne often disagreed with Palmerston's methods, he instinctively believed that 'all party arrangements' appeared 'infinitely small' in

---

[63] John Prest, *Lord John Russell* (Columbia, SC, 1972), pp. 305–6; *Lady John Russell. A Memoir*, ed. Desmond MacCarthy and Agatha Russell (New York, 1911), p. 105; B.L., LP (3) 42, no. 29: Palmerston to Lansdowne, 31 Oct. 1849; Russell to Lansdowne, 26 Oct. 1852, in Gooch, *Later Russell Correspondence*, II, 109.

[64] Hansard, *Parl. Debs.*, 3rd ser., XCVIII, 690–1, 5 May 1848; B.L., LP (3) 43: Russell to Lansdowne, 29 Mar. 1848; P.R.O., 30/22/7C, ff. 359–60: Lansdowne to Russell, [May 1848]; B.L., LP (3) 42, no. 23: Palmerston to Lansdowne, 5 May 1848; B.L., LP (3) 31, no. 28: Clarendon to Lansdowne, 9, 12, 13 May 1848; *Greville Memoirs*, VI, 60–1.

[65] Evelyn Ashley, *The Life of Henry John Temple, Viscount Palmerston, 1846–1865* (2 vols, 1876), II, 1–4.

[66] Gray, *Famine, Land and Politics*, pp. 148, 185–9; B.L., LP (3) 42, no. 29: Palmerston to Lansdowne, 31 Oct. 1849; B.L., LP (3) 43: Russell to Lansdowne, 9 Dec. 1851; Palmerston to Russell, 10 Dec. 1851, in Gooch, *Later Russell Correspondence*, I, 216, II, 125–27; Stuart J. Reid, *Lord Palmerston* (1892), pp. 153–7; Donald Southgate, *The Most English Minister* (1966), pp. 310–12; 22 Dec. 1853, in *Disraeli, Derby and the Conservative Party. Journals and Memoirs of Edward Henry, Lord Stanley, 1849–1864*, ed. John Vincent (New York, 1978), p. 114.

the face of political instability abroad.⁶⁷ In these circumstances, it is impossible to say with certainty when Lansdowne was working on behalf of party, state, or individual conscience. Russell's tendency to develop domestic policy without consultation and Palmerston's proclivity for *imperium* at the foreign office made it difficult to know exactly what constituted the 'government's business' and what was the personal fiat of a minister.

Given Lansdowne's frequent rebellion against Russell's more advanced measures, the two remained on remarkably cordial terms.⁶⁸ This in part reflected their shared heritage and good manners, but they also each understood the peculiar circumstances of the other House. Russell, for instance, argued in favour of the resolution against Peel's 'miserable' Corn Bill in 1842 in the Commons, but recognized that for whig Lords, it was 'quite another matter'. There they might legitimately vote in favour of the second reading as 'the present bill makes some little improvement on the existing system'.⁶⁹ Russell routinely consulted Lansdowne regarding personnel matters, and they worked together to summon cabinets, develop strategy and bring legislation forward in their respective Houses. It appears that Henry Tufnell, head whip in the Commons and a protégé of Lansdowne's, was used by both Russell and Lansdowne for issuing cabinet and general summonses.⁷⁰ With a legislative logjam in late 1847, Lansdowne and Russell together arranged to move a committee on bank regulations, have it meet in order to call for papers, then adjourn until the new year when they could 'secure an attendance'.⁷¹ Lansdowne and Russell agreed in 1848 that the bill for establishing diplomatic relations with Rome should originate in the Lords in February 1848, and arranged to give 'some length of notice', because Lansdowne did not wish to take the House by surprise, and because Strafford recommended 'a little time to get our attendance'. Lansdowne also wrote circulars to peers who had not taken their seats.⁷²

Lansdowne's reputation and social position enabled him to facilitate the larger, constitutional process of government in which success was measured in terms of the smooth interaction of all parts of the mixed constitution. While his laxity regarding observance of strict party lines had in the past worked against him in a party sense, in the confused political conditions after 1846 he was uniquely suited to work with parties and politicians in both Houses, and with the queen. Lansdowne showed the utmost respect for Wellington and Stanley, going out of his way to accommodate absences and delays, and co-operating in the scheduling of motions and committee meetings. His reputation for conciliation and fair play earned him a measure of consideration that sometimes worked to whig advantage. In 1850, for instance, Stanley was twice

---

⁶⁷ P.R.O., 30/22/9J(2), f. 60: Lansdowne to Russell, 18 Dec. 1851.

⁶⁸ The best brief account of Russell's ability to simultaneously inspire respect and raise concern among his colleagues is J. P. Parry, 'Past and Future in the Later Career of Lord John Russell', in *History and Biography. Essays in Honour of Derek Beales*, ed. T. C. W. Blanning and David Cannadine (Cambridge, 1996), pp. 152–6.

⁶⁹ B.L., LP (3) 43: Russell to Lansdowne, 11 Mar. 1842.

⁷⁰ P.R.O., 30/22/5G, ff. 202–3: Lansdowne to Russell, [1846]; P.R.O., 30/22/5G, ff. 169–70: Lansdowne to Russell, [1846].

⁷¹ B.L., LP, (3) 43: Lansdowne to Russell, [late 1847].

⁷² P.R.O., 30/22/7A, f. 250: Lansdowne to Russell, [Feb. 1848].

persuaded to postpone inquiry into the Don Pacifico matter, affording time for the whigs to develop 'a satisfactory answer'.[73] In the first instance, Stanley had only given notice the night before, and therefore might have been put off by anyone. On 6 June, however, Lansdowne called his reputation into play. With 'great reluctance', he asked on 'his responsibility as a minister' for delay, arguing that a discussion at that moment might lead to 'injurious consequences' when 'communications' with France were expected to lead to a satisfactory resolution of the problem.[74] Lansdowne also served as liaison between party leaders when they sat in different Houses. In 1847, for instance, Stanley was willing to allow extension of the poor law to Ireland if substantial concessions were made to landowners. Russell tried to gain concessions by suggesting in the Commons that the government might entertain clauses that they did not intend to propose. While praising Lansdowne for conducting negotiations 'with so complete an absence of all party feeling', he complained loudly of Russell's breach of the implicit bipartisanship that had theretofore prevailed.[75]

In many periods of parliamentary politics, an 'absence of party feeling' would not have been considered a highly desirable quality. In the turbulence of the 1840s and 1850s, it made sense, and it ensured that Lansdowne would be remembered for more than good manners and a dutiful superintendence of the Lords under Russell. What set Lansdowne apart from previous whig leaders in the house of lords was the combination of a willingness to do the procedural work, the skills to do it well, and an enormous fund of experience and dignity. He had in fact been leading in some capacity in the house of lords since 1809, and as a result enjoyed a stature very near that of a former prime minister. Nominally Lansdowne's superior, Russell never attempted to force him except insofar as reason and argument could effect a change of position, and he frequently deferred to his 'oldest and closest political friend'.[76] Lansdowne was so useful in working the Lords, and so ready to assent to general principles of political and Irish reforms, that Russell must have convinced himself that his elder colleague could be persuaded on the details as well. It was always 'next session' for the great reform bill that never came. Governing is, however, about more than major reform legislation. Maintaining the government for six years, under the most trying circumstances both domestically and internationally, was a considerable achievement. In that time, Lansdowne demonstrated that moderates – be they whig, tory or Peelite – were good guardians of the public trust, and that the country had no need for 'such men as Bright and Cobden'.[77] Lansdowne was the outstanding example of a party leader who actually operated outside the spirit of party, who believed that the 'principle of Coalitions' was 'not only just, but necessary in a free country'.

---

[73] P.R.O., 30/22/7B, f. 288: Lansdowne to Russell, [?14 Apr. 1848]; *Greville Memoirs*, VI, 211; Durham Univ. Lib, GRE/B113/4B/39: Lansdowne to Grey, [rcd. 11 Apr. 1850]. See too P.R.O., 30/22/7B, f. 288: Lansdowne to Russell, [Apr. 1848].

[74] Hansard, *Parl. Debs*, CXI, 798, 6 June 1850.

[75] B.L., LP (3) 7: Derby to Lansdowne, 12 Mar. 1847; LP (3) 43, no. 43: Russell to Lansdowne, 15 Mar. 1847; Gray, *Famine, Land and Politics*, pp. 276–83.

[76] Walpole, *Life of Russell*, II, 200.

[77] *Disraeli, Derby and the Conservative Party*, ed. Vincent, p. 54.

'A Host in Himself': Lord Derby and Aristocratic Leadership

ANGUS HAWKINS

Few Conservative leaders have retired at moments of their own choosing. Many have been pushed; few have jumped. Most recently Edward Heath, Margaret Thatcher and John Major, like their predecessors Arthur Balfour and Neville Chamberlain, have relinquished their leadership nursing a bitter sense of betrayal. Most Conservative leaders, moreover, have come to harbour a private degree of contempt for those under their command. Sir Robert Peel's disdain for his Conservative backbenchers was apparent before and obvious after the brutal party schism of 1846. Benjamin Disraeli retained a life-long sense that the tory squires were undeserving of his talent. Lord Salisbury too had scant regard for the Conservative rank and file in the Commons. Devotion and ruthlessness conspire around the brittle entity of party leadership. While some, such as Lord Kilmuir in the 1960s, have claimed loyalty and unity as the ascendant virtues of the Conservative party, many of the party's leaders have faced a rather harsher and more unforgiving reality.[1]

A select few Conservative leaders have enjoyed sustained and largely unquestioned support. Lord Salisbury comes immediately to mind. The fourteenth earl of Derby, Conservative leader for 22 years from 1846 to 1868, is another member of this fortunate select group.[2] Until severe illness finally forced his retirement in February 1868, Derby headed a party for longer than any other politician in modern British politics, unchallenged by a serious rival or any substantial desertion of support. Nor, unlike Peel or Disraeli, did Derby nurture a private antipathy towards those who offered him their allegiance. Between 1846 and 1868 Derby was the undisputed head of his party. As such he became the first British statesman to become prime minister three times, in 1852, 1858 and 1866. He did not, like Peel, lead his party to rupture. Nor was his authority, like that of Disraeli's, a flimsy craft negotiating powerful undercurrents of suspicion and distrust. As a member of the house of lords Derby steered the Conservatives from the debilitating crisis over corn law repeal through to the second parliamentary Reform Act. He restored the rank and file remnants of Peel's Conservative party as a credible national body capable of assuming office. By doing so he gave the party a future. No Conservative leader, after 1835 and before

---

[1] John Ramsden, *An Appetite for Power. A History of the Conservative Party Since 1830* (1998), p. 51. This essay was written before the general election and Conservative leadership contest of 2001; events which gave little cause to revise these opening comments.

[2] For convenience I have referred to Derby throughout this essay by his final title. From 1834 to 1844 he was Lord Stanley. In 1844 he was elevated to the Lords as Lord Stanley of Bickerstaffe, and in 1851 he succeeded his father as the 14th earl of Derby.

1997, inherited a weaker hand. All too easily the Conservatives, shorn of Peelite talent and experience, might have lapsed into an atavistic rump of rural protest. The party's survival was Derby's own achievement.

That achievement has many aspects. Understanding the complexity of Derby's career, his political doctrine, constitutional principles, social philosophy and religious beliefs, engages a number of differing viewpoints. His limitations and weaknesses as a politician, as well as his susceptibility to depression and recurrent periods of serious illness, sit alongside his strengths and abilities.[3] This essay examines just one facet of Derby's career. As a peer, what was the nature of his party leadership? What strategies and methods enabled him to preserve party unity and to restore Conservative credibility? This focus, in turn, throws light on the status and influence of the house of lords in mid-Victorian politics.

As historians have increasingly come to appreciate, the 1832 Reform Act did not emasculate the Lords, rendering it passively subservient to the elected Commons.[4] Political leaders such as the second Earl Grey, for the whigs, and the duke of Wellington, for the Conservatives, saw the Lords as playing an active and effective role in the governing of the nation. Walter Bagehot in his classic description of the mid-Victorian polity, published in book form in 1867 as *The English Constitution*, suggested that the house of lords, because it represented only the interests of the landowning aristocracy, was relegated after 1832 to a subordinate constitutional function. But Bagehot's analysis understated the importance of the upper House in the workings of the mid-Victorian political system. The formal powers of the Lords, which still possessed an unlimited right to veto legislation, remained unchanged after 1832. Moreover, as Bagehot acknowledged, the upper House provided a 'reservoir' of cabinet ministers.[5] In 1863, for example, the foreign office, the colonial office, the war office and the admiralty were all headed by peers sitting in the Lords. Like Lord Aberdeen from 1852 to 1855, as premier in 1852, 1858–9 and 1866–8, Derby led his governments as a member of the upper House. Derby's Conservative leadership from 1846 to 1868 comprises an important part of the continued aristocratic influence on Victorian party politics, connecting the era of Wellington to the heyday of the third marquis of Salisbury during the 1880s and 1890s.

The constitutional context for Derby's leadership was shaped by the conventions of 'parliamentary government'.[6] Mid-Victorian parliamentary parties were voluntary associations of like-minded individuals. As Derby himself described them in 1854,

---

[3] A fuller biographical study of Derby is forthcoming in Angus Hawkins, *The Forgotten Prime Minister. A Political Portrait of the 14th Earl of Derby, 1799–1869*. See also Angus Hawkins, 'Lord Derby and Victorian Conservatism: A Reappraisal.' *Parliamentary History*, VI (1987), and 'Lord Derby' in *Lords of Parliament. Studies, 1714–1914*, ed. R. W. Davis (Stanford, 1995), pp. 134–62.

[4] See, for example, *Lords of Parliament*, ed. Davis, and E. A. Smith, *The House of Lords in British Politics and Society, 1815–1911* (1992).

[5] W. Bagehot *The English Constitution*, ed. Paul Smith (Cambridge, 2001), p. 10. As well as the valuable introduction provided by Paul Smith to this edition, see the discussion of Bagehot in T. A. Jenkins, *Parliament, Party and Politics in Victorian Britain* (Manchester, 1996), pp. 11–12.

[6] See Angus Hawkins, '"Parliamentary Government" and Victorian Political Parties c.1830–c.1880.' *English Historical Review*, CIV (1989), 630–69, and Angus Hawkins, *British Party Politics, 1852–1886* (1998), pp. 9–46.

parties were made up of those in the habit of acting together.[7] The habit of association drew on family connexions, tradition, friendship and partisan feeling, as well as shared ideas. Those means of ensuring strict party discipline available to later leaders, however, were lacking. In his appeals to his party followers, either individually or collectively, Derby disavowed any wish to force them to act contrary to their conscientious convictions. In part this was a recognition of the fact that Commons M.P.s owed their electoral success to local constituency support, rather than the endorsement of national party organizations which, by the 1880s, were enjoying a centralised bureaucracy and popular membership. Consent, not coercion, cemented party affiliation in parliament. Derby always addressed his party supporters as 'his friends', rather than as enlisted subordinates. Allegiance was solicitously sought not demanded. In turn, this required that, on occasion, party leaders be prepared to follow rather than direct party sentiment. In 1847 Derby advised Lord George Bentinck that 'Peel's great error has always been disregarding the opinion of his party, whenever it did not exactly square with his own: and I am confident that no man in these days can hope to lead a party who cannot make up his mind sometimes to follow it.'[8] As Derby's eldest son observed in his journal; 'a party could not be disciplined like a regiment'.[9]

This produced parliamentary parties sufficiently cohesive to endorse government authority without reliance on the prerogative. Equally, it ensured that party connexions were sufficiently loose as to guard against governments being directly dependent upon an electoral mandate. It was the dynamics of party association within Westminster, not the monarch or the people, that determined who governed. Between 1835 and 1868 only one ministry not in a substantial Commons minority, Lord Melbourne's government in 1841, was brought down in a straight party contest, rather than by intra-party conflict. This was not politics in the absence of party, but politics expressed through parties of a kind intrinsic to parliamentary government. Parties were cohesive, but not rigid. Every parliament elected between 1841 and 1868 brought down at least one, if not two, governments during its lifetime. Sovereignty resided in parliament, not with the crown or with the electorate. Changes of government were not aligned with general elections. Parliament itself made and unmade ministries. This reinforced the nature of parliamentary parties as voluntary associations, in fulfilment of their essential constitutional function as the guardians of parliamentary sovereignty.

Party cohesion, therefore, was crucially dependent upon personal loyalty to the party leader. In this regard Derby's credentials were impeccable. As a landed aristocrat, with country habits and debating skill, Derby possessed a natural parliamentary authority. He did not have the commercial origins of Peel, or the urban literary background of Disraeli who never learnt to ride a horse. Instead, the broad acres of

---

[7] Liverpool R.O., Derby MSS 920 DER(14) 182/2: Derby to Blandford, 26 Jan. 1854. I am grateful to the earl of Derby for his kind permission to quote from the Derby MSS.

[8] Derby MSS 920 DER(14) 172/2: Derby to Bentinck, 27 Oct. 1847 cited. Robert Stewart, *The Politics of Protection. Lord Derby and the Protectionist Party, 1841–1852* (Cambridge, 1971), p. 222. See also P. M. Gurowich, 'Party and Independence in the Early and Mid-Victorian House of Commons', University of Cambridge Ph.D., 1986.

[9] *Disraeli, Derby and the Conservative Party. The Political Journals of Lord Stanley 1849–69.* ed. J. Vincent (Hassocks, 1978), p. 103.

the Knowsley estate, outside Liverpool, the patronage of seven anglican livings in Lancashire, Cheshire and Yorkshire, and a title going back to 1485, complemented Derby's private passion for field and turf. In 1846 the Conservative party was the representation of the landed interest and the established Church. Derby personified the privileged historic status of aristocratic anglican landownership. Conservative affection for Derby cemented party loyalty. In 1861 the *Illustrated London News* observed that Derby was 'nearly adored by all his party'.[10] Similarly, a Conservative former M.P. confirmed to the Commons chief whip that 'what has kept the party together' was 'the influence and most successful leadership of Lord Derby', the Conservatives having 'gone to all lengths to support Lord Derby because we loved and trusted him as a leader'.[11]

To a party stripped in 1846 of talent, administrative expertise and debaters, Derby also brought widely-recognised ability. He provided not only a fitting focus for party loyalty, but much needed experience and capability. Derby's resignation from Peel's cabinet in December 1845, in protest at the proposed repeal of the corn laws, was a critical moment for the future of the Conservative party. Derby's final comment in Peel's cabinet was that 'we cannot do this as gentlemen'; repeal violated the trust placed in the party leadership by the parliamentary rank and file.[12] By abandoning Peel in 1845 Derby became available as a respectable leader for the protectionists after 1846. (Although his vote against repeal of the corn laws was a difficult choice between the lesser of evils, arrived at only after much soul searching.) In the Commons, prior to 1844, Derby had acquired a reputation as one of the foremost orators of his day. During the reform debates of 1831–2, as a member of Lord Grey's government, he had laid claim to 'the palm of eloquence'. In 1829 William Huskisson called him 'the Hope of the Nation'.[13] He was hailed in his youth, having won the chancellor's prize for Latin composition in 1819 while up at Oxford, as the only brilliant eldest son produced by the British peerage for 100 years.[14] A keen intelligence lay behind the bluff reserve and patrician aloofness that kept many at a distance. For Derby had 'no intimates, except the sharers of his amusements'.[15] But in private Disraeli marvelled at Derby's capability; 'his mind always clear, his patience extraordinary, he rises in difficulty, and his resources never fail'.[16] The Conservative minister and novelist Edward Bulwer Lytton thought Derby 'the *cleverest* public man he had ever met'.[17] The whig lord chancellor, Lord Campbell, declared Derby to be 'a host in himself. He has a marvellous acuteness of intellect and consummate powers in debate. There is no subject which he cannot master thoroughly and lucidly explain.'[18]

---

[10] *The Illustrated London News*, 15 June 1861.

[11] Somerset R.O., Hylton MSS DD/HY/24/107: ? to Jolliffe, 22 Nov. 1859.

[12] Lord Broughton, *Recollections of a Long Life*, ed. Lady Dorchester (6 vols, 1909–11), VI, 229.

[13] W. D. Jones, *Lord Derby and Victorian Conservatism* (Oxford, 1956), p. 18.

[14] *Ibid.*, p. 6.

[15] *Disraeli's Reminiscences*, ed. H. M. Swartz and M. Swartz (1975), p. 124.

[16] *Disraeli, Derby and the Conservative Party*, ed. Vincent, p. 72.

[17] Hertfordshire R.O., Lytton MSS, C 13, f. 21: Lytton memo., n.d. [1869].

[18] M. S. Hardcastle, *The Life of John, Lord Campbell, Lord High Chancellor of Great Britain* (2 vols, 1881), II, 324.

Some contemporaries, offended by Derby's *insouciant* air, and later historians, confusing manner with motivation, have taken Derby's expressions of personal indifference to political success as indications of idleness, irresponsibility and lack of ambition. Derby's passion for horse racing has been cited as proof that he was, in truth, a dilettante. An inappropriate levity, it is suggested, fatally marred his abilities. Lord Campbell remembered 'the excessive *brusquerie*' of Derby's manner with strangers, and 'his carelessness about the opinion of others'.[19] But a demeanour of patrician detachment was entirely characteristic to one of Derby's background and aristocratic status. As was observed of Lord Melbourne in 1851, 'light indifference – a sort of disdainful carelessness', was the 'ordinary habit' of aristocrats and of 'almost all who desire to assume the tone of high society'.[20] Political office was portrayed as an onerous public obligation, not a valued prize striven for with obvious earnestness. Derby's forays to Epsom and Newmarket during the parliamentary session were not symptoms of a lack of political commitment. Nor were a formal public pose of lofty indifference to personal advancement or expressions of selfless devotion to the national interest reliable indications of private purpose. Political rhetoric serves to persuade not explain.

Derby's private correspondence reveals that a public principled disinterestedness cloaked a genuine dedication to party success in Westminster. Just as his carefully penned memoranda on administrative aspects of government revealed a high seriousness. To act independently of party, he declared, was to be 'either useless or dangerous'.[21] As he lectured Disraeli in January 1849:[22] 'He who has once put his hand to the parliamentary plough cannot draw back … [T]hose whom talent, or station, or accident, has placed in the foreground and enabled them to exercise, whether they will or no, an influence over numbers of their brother members [,] for them there is no retreat.' The conventional pose of patriotic detachment from narrow partisan purpose, rebuffing imputations of faction, was the acceptable public face of a sincere personal commitment to party advantage. Appearances belied a firm determination. 'I have nothing at heart', he declared, 'but the support of the views which I entertain in public affairs and as a means to that end the maintenance of union and *Party*.'[23] Even when in low spirits, as in December 1852 following his ejection from office, Derby's commitment to the political fight remained: 'the game is lost, but I think it ought to be played, and I will play it out to the end'.[24]

If public expressions of disinterestedness are misleading guides to Derby's real purposes, his illness and susceptibility to depression are important factors in understanding his leadership fully. Derby's periodic attacks of severe gout, which confined him to his sickbed, have been noted by historians and added to his limitations as a party leader. But the difficulties of Derby's health were more extensive and complex

---

[19] *Ibid.*, II, 87.

[20] W. Johnstone, *England As It Is* (2 vols, 1851), I, 122, 126; see Gurowich, 'Party and Independence', pp. 205–9.

[21] Derby MSS 920 DER(14) 178/1: Derby to Herries, 6 Jan. 1849.

[22] Derby to Disraeli, 6 Jan. 1849, cited in W. F. Monypenny and G. E. Buckle, *The Life of Benjamin Disraeli, Earl of Beaconsfield* (6 vols, 1910–20), III, 127.

[23] *Ibid.*, p. 128.

[24] *Disraeli, Derby and the Conservative Party*, ed. Vincent, p. 94.

than occasional confinement. Derby suffered his first serious attack of gout at the age of 34, after serving as chief secretary for Ireland in Lord Grey's cabinet. A genetic predisposition to the disease, triggered by a severe bout of influenza, was aggravated by the extraordinary exertion and stress of the preceding three years, combating Daniel O'Connell in parliament, imposing the rule of law in Ireland, and taking a leading part in securing the successful passage of the 1832 Reform Act. Thereafter, attacks of gout, bringing excruciating pain, rendered him an invalid for prolonged periods throughout his life.

But as well as chronic physical illness, Derby was also prey to periods of deep depression. By the 1840s these dark periods of depression descended upon him with a cyclical regularity. In the first half of each year, during the exhilaration of the session and the main racing calendar, he was usually active and resolute. By the beginning of the recess, during July and August, this buoyant mood normally gave way to despondency, gloom and a pervasive melancholy. Irritable apprehension and pessimistic fatalism were then exacerbated by recurrent attacks of gout. Not until December and January did this depression usually lift, accompanied by the recovery of his physical health and mental vigour. This annual pattern of activeness, followed by deep depression, was also a genetic disposition. Derby's father had fought his prolonged periods of reclusive melancholy by immersion in zoological study. Both Derby's sons suffered from what they called 'black dog'; an enervating periodic sense of impending calamity brought on by inaction after great exertion, which they recognized in the psychology of their father.[25] 1853 and 1856, following the excitements of 1852 and 1855, were particularly bad years for Derby when depression dogged him almost constantly. In other years January to June usually saw him deliver in Westminster memorable parliamentary performances reviving memories of the triumphs of his youth; resolute activity then giving way to despondent invalidity during the autumn in the political remoteness of his Lancashire estate. Yet, even when brought low by illness and depression, Derby remained committed to the political battle in Westminster and the Conservative cause.

When Derby reflected, during the late 1840s, on the eventual alignment of parliamentary opinion likely to emerge from the dislocation of parties created in 1846, he anticipated a fundamental struggle between democratic and aristocratic principles. How, in the aftermath of 1846, were the urban middle-classes to align themselves in a society experiencing political flux? The advance of free trade policies, he observed in August 1850, had lowered the weight of proprietors of the soil in the social scale and threatened a rapid slide towards 'a republic in name as well as in reality'.[26] This would forge, he predicted, a future union between Conservatives and moderate whigs. The Peelites, meanwhile, would increasingly embrace populism. The 'scattered remnants of the Peelites' he regarded as 'the most dangerous men'.[27] Peel's own disregard for party in parliament, which rendered him 'the apostle of expediency', would lead to a dangerous and unrestrained populism and their acceptance of congenial

---

[25] Derby MSS: journal of 15th earl of Derby, 17 Nov. 1878. I am grateful to Professor John Vincent for this reference.
[26] Derby to Croker, 18 Aug. 1850, cited in L. J. Jennings *The Croker Papers* (3 vols, 1884), III, 217–8.
[27] *Ibid.*, p. 219.

company amongst the radicals. Whigs such as Lords Lansdowne, Minto, Grey and Granville, in contrast, retained a belief in landed aristocratic government which suggested a fundamental compatibility with the Conservatives. Such thinking, in the late 1840s, was a remarkable forecast of that realignment of party opinion which occurred after 1886, when moderate whigs such as Lord Hartington merged with the Conservative party, in reaction to Gladstone's populist campaign for Irish home rule. In the late 1840s such ideas reinforced Derby's own firm conviction that an alliance of non-Conservative opinion, embracing whigs, Liberals, Peelites and radicals, was unsustainable. Increasingly during the 1850s Derby saw moderate whigs, rather than prominent Peelites such as Sir James Graham, Sidney Herbert and Edward Cardwell, as the best prospect for adhesion to the Conservatives. He was prepared to discuss reunion with individual Peelites such as William Gladstone. Indeed, between 1846 and 1859 a total of 71 backbench Peelite M.P.s quietly rejoined the Conservative party. But the Peelite leadership he came to regard as a lost cause. 'We have nothing to look to from the *leading* Peelites', Derby concluded in February 1851, 'but rancorous opposition.'[28] Rather, by way of reaction, democratic pressure would foster a fusion of 'real Conservatives, whether nominal Tory or nominal Whig'.[29]

The preservation of aristocratic government required the maintenance of the house of lords as an efficient part of the parliamentary system. Derby's view of the appropriate relationship between the Commons and Lords was clear. 'The House of Commons is the best *originator* and the House of Lords the best *reviser* of legislative measures.'[30] If the Lords lost its ability to challenge the Commons then the government would be defenceless against the tyranny of party opinion in the lower House. In response to the popular radical criticism of aristocratic government inflamed by the mismanagement of the Crimean war, Derby expounded to a Liverpool audience in October 1855 the virtues of the house of lords. The upper House, he pronounced, 'performed an important and useful function in checking hasty legislation', while presenting 'no barrier to freedom and improvement'.[31] The British peerage was not a closed caste, but by infusions of new blood was open to those who showed themselves worthy of entering that distinguished assembly. At the same time, Derby exercised his greatest influence in the Lords when championing its privileges, traditions and constitutional rights. Most famously, in 1856 Derby successfully galvanized Lords opposition to Lord Palmerston's proposal to elevate the lawyer Sir James Parke as Lord Wensleydale with a life peerage. Controversial life peerages, as opposed to hereditary titles, Derby argued, threatened the historic independence of the Lords, subordinating the upper House to both crown and Commons, and disrupting the 1688 settlement of constitutional checks and balances. Life peerages would constitute a political bait dangled before father and son to keep a family loyal to the government, thereby subverting the independence of the Lords.

---

[28] Derby MSS 920 DER(14) 179/1: Derby to Malmesbury, 15 Feb. 1851. For an identification of those free trade Conservatives who rejoined Derby's party after 1846 see Gurowich 'Party and Independence', pp. 370–2.

[29] Derby to Croker, 18 Aug. 1850, cited in Jennings, *Croker Papers*, III, 218.

[30] Derby MSS. 920 DER(14) 178/1: Derby to Shaw-Lefevre, 29 Mar. 1848.

[31] *The Times*, 11 Oct. 1855.

As a practical matter, however, Derby always sought to avoid, as far as was responsibly possible, a direct clash between the two Houses. Over the Wensleydale peerage Derby steered Lords opposition towards a compromise. It was bitter hostility towards Palmerston in the Commons, not aristocratic reactionaryism, which finally killed off the attempt to create Parke a life peer with a right to sit in the Lords.[32] Similarly, as prime minister in 1858, Derby avoided an imminent collision between the Commons and Lords over the admission of Jews to parliament. Lord John Russell's bill to amend the parliamentary oath, so as to allow Baron Lionel de Rothschild to take his seat as M.P. for the City of London, was approved by the Commons. The Lords had already vetoed this proposal twice before during the 1850s. In April 1858 Russell's bill was again rejected by the Lords and a confrontation between the two Houses appeared inevitable. Derby, however, immediately engineered a compromise so as to 'save the dignity, and to a certain extent maintain the principles, of both Houses'.[33] Each House was enabled to alter the parliamentary oath with regard to its own members. Thus a dangerous constitutional crisis was adeptly avoided.

The skilful management of Lords support was the more important to Derby because he lacked an automatic majority. He effectively controlled the election of the 16 Scottish and 28 Irish representative peers.[34] But the presence of Peelite peers after 1846, led by Lord Aberdeen, as well as the Liberal peers led first by Lord Lansdowne and then by Lord Granville, denied him the natural Lords majority enjoyed by Wellington. In May 1846 91 Conservative peers had supported Peel and Wellington, while 146 Conservative peers followed Derby in opposing corn law repeal. That the ecclesiastical lords, 26 bishops and archbishops from the Church of England and four from the Church of Ireland, were often reluctant to follow Derby's lead after 1846 exacerbated these difficulties. By 1850 Derby estimated that there were about 40 Peelite peers, who often held the balance of power.[35] Thus Derby devoted considerable time and energy to marshalling support in the upper House. Lords Malmesbury and Eglinton served as Derby's whips in the Lords after 1846, the Irish peer the third earl of Desart supporting their work after 1848. Lord Redesdale, Wellington's former chief whip in the Lords, provided advice. But it was the services of the conscientious and judicious Lord Colville, as his chief whip in the Lords after 1852, that was a great assistance to Derby in playing a weakened hand. Colville was assisted after 1852 by the young fourth marquess of Bath, whose hospitality at Longleat and contributions to Conservative election funds were offset by his vanity and fondness for drink. The organization of proxy votes, a facility unavailable in the Commons, as well as the pairing of votes used in both Houses, was a constant

---

[32] See Olive Anderson, 'The Wensleydale Peerage Case and the Position of the House of Lords in the Mid-Nineteenth Century', *English Historical Review*, LXXXII (1967), 486–502.

[33] The marquess of Salisbury, Hatfield House, Hertfordshire, Salisbury MSS: Derby memo., 9 June 1858. See also Derby MSS 920 DER(14) 184/1: Derby to Lyndhurst, 13 June 1858.

[34] One disgruntled Irish Liberal peer complained that the representative peerages 'were made in Lord Derby's drawing room'. In 1867 Granville declared that Derby 'has a power almost superior to the Queen's prerogative of making peers, by practically having the selection of the Scotch and Irish representative peers'. Smith, *House of Lords*, p. 79.

[35] Derby MSS 920 DER(14) 178/2: Derby to Exeter, 13 Apr. 1850.

labour.³⁶ During the session circulars requesting attendance at important divisions were sent out, with separate circulars sent to dukes. Recognizing his weak claim upon their loyalty Derby usually refrained from communicating with the bishops, preferring to be seen to leave their votes to their unfettered consciences. Management of the Irish representative peerage, meanwhile, also demanded Derby's attention. In 1865, for example, Derby became directly involved in keeping the wayward Lord Powerscourt in line. 'Nothing can be more shifty and less satisfactory' than Powerscourt's behaviour, Derby complained, it being 'utterly inconsistent with the understanding on which he was selected.'³⁷ Noting the fragile health of elderly peers with eldest sons in the Commons, as in the cases of Lord Warwick in 1853 and Lord Aberdeen in 1860, comprised a further aspect of his shepherding of Lords support. After 1858 these labours were repaid with Derby enjoying a stronger control over Conservative peers, in part because a number of Peelite peers had rejoined his party. The three large-scale Lords votes after 1859, on the Paper Duties Bill in May 1860, the Danish censure motion of July 1864, and the Roman Catholic Oath Bill of June 1865, all resulted in opposition victories over the government. In June 1859 the Liberal leader in the Lords, Granville, reported to Palmerston that 'the close attendance of [Derby's] supporters both in and out of office was very remarkable. This was probably owing not merely to a stricter system of discipline, which is characteristic of the Conservative party, but also to the great personal ascendancy of [Derby], and his position as prime minister.'³⁸

Between 1846 and 1867 Derby voted in 180 Lords divisions. In 24 divisions he supported the government and in another 64 divisions he lost the vote. Victory in 92 divisions represented a far from negligible achievement in the circumstances. Often the divisions were close. On a number of crucial occasions they were only lost on proxy votes. Derby's major assault against Russell's government in 1849, over repeal of the Navigation Acts, secured a majority of those present in the chamber. But 68 proxy votes recorded for the ministry resulted in his defeat. Derby's greatest successes, when he amassed a powerful Lords majority, came in 1850, over the 'Don Pacifico' affair, and in 1860, when Gladstone's proposal to abolish the paper duties was rejected. In one of the greatest oratorical performances of the period, Derby opposed on 17 June 1850 Palmerston's foreign policy. Even the unsympathetic young Liberal peer, Lord Wodehouse, regarded Derby's statement as 'the most brilliant speech I think I ever heard'.³⁹ In a packed chamber, for three hours, Derby denounced, as 'the prodigality of folly', a policy which had prostituted the authority of a great nation to the enforcement of unjust demands upon a weak and defenceless Greece. Malmesbury described the speech in one word, 'magnificent'.⁴⁰ Derby secured a majority of 37 peers, defeating the government by 169 to 132 votes. Only an equally

---

³⁶ See J. Hogan, 'Party Management in the House of Lords, 1846–1865', *Parliamentary History*, X (1991), 124–50.

³⁷ Derby MSS 920 DER(14) 190/1: Derby to Rokeby, 8 Nov. 1865, and Derby to Drogheda, 5 Nov. 1865.

³⁸ Southampton U.L., Broadlands MSS GC/GR/1863: Granville to Palmerston, 18 June 1859.

³⁹ *The Journal of John Wodehouse, First Earl of Kimberley for 1862–1902*, ed. Angus Hawkins and John Powell (Camden 5th ser., IX 1997), pp. 44–5.

⁴⁰ Lord Malmesbury, *Memoirs of an Ex-Minister* (2 vols 1884), I, 263.

brilliant performance on 25 June by Palmerston in the Commons, in an epic speech of four and three quarter hours culminating in the resonant phrase *Civis Romanus sum*, saved the ministry. In 1860 Derby skilfully exploited the divisions within Palmerston's cabinet over Gladstone's financial policy to lead the Lords to a rejection of abolition of the paper duties. Derby was well aware that the prime minister was, at best, lukewarm about his chancellor's proposal. In response to the government defeat Palmerston referred the question of whether the Lords could reject a finance bill approved by the Commons to a committee of privileges. The report of the Committee, that the Lords did have such power, was presented to the Commons by Palmerston in July 1860, the premier allowing himself in his speech to imply personal reservations about the merits of Gladstone's budget. This was the fulfilment of Derby's opposition strategy, as Lord Malmesbury described it, of keeping 'the cripples on their legs'.[41]

For 18 of his 22 years of Conservative leadership Derby headed a party in opposition. Just as convention required of prominent politicians a public pose of no interest in office, so it was essential for an opposition to be seen to be eschewing faction and giving the queen's government a 'fair trial'. An opposition must seem unafraid of office, while not appearing eager to seize it. As Derby advised the Conservative M.P. Sir John Pakington in November 1865, it was necessary in speeches to 'disclaim any factious opposition or desire to embarrass ministers'.[42] Such conventional sentiment was not, as it has often been understood, a symptom of Derby's private belief 'that office was scarcely a prize to be sought and the apprehension that in office the Conservatives had little that was distinctive to offer the nation'.[43] Rather, public expressions of patriotic detachment served to enhance statesmanlike claims to office. 'By this disinterested kind of language', Derby candidly observed in 1849, 'I am much more likely to secure a young man than if I showed eagerness to get his vote.'[44]

Such language complemented Derby's consistent opposition strategy of 'masterly inactivity';[45] Conservative passivity allowing whig, Liberal, Peelite and radical differences to come to the fore. Derby was 'well aware of what is said of the necessity of having some "watchword" or "party cry"'.[46] But he was equally aware of the effect that Conservative initiatives while in opposition could have in consolidating opponents against them. '[T]o foment divisions and jealousies in the government majority must be our first objective', Derby explained to Disraeli in 1857, 'while we should carefully avoid multiplying occasions for their voting in concert, in opposition to motions brought forward by us.'[47] This strategy echoed Peel's opposition policy of the late 1830s and that adopted by the whigs between 1841–6. In opposition between 1846 and 1866 Derby consistently pursued a line of 'masterly inactivity' designed to foment internal divisions amongst those arrayed against him. In November 1855 even the restless Disraeli acknowledged that 'silence and inertia are our wisest course';[48]

---

[41] *Ibid.*, II, 215.
[42] Derby MSS 920 DER(14) 190/1: Derby to Pakington, 10 Nov. 1865.
[43] Robert Stewart, *The Foundation of the Conservative Party, 1830–1867* (1978), p. 223.
[44] *Disraeli, Derby and the Conservative Party*, ed. Vincent, p. 4.
[45] Derby to Malmesbury, 4 Dec. 1860, cited in Malmesbury, *Memoirs*, II, 242.
[46] Derby to Disraeli, 22 Sept. 1849, cited in Monypenny and Buckle, *Disraeli*, III, 215.
[47] Derby to Disraeli, 24 Apr. 1857, cited in *ibid.*, IV, 80.
[48] Derby MSS 920 DER(14) 145/3: Disraeli to Derby, 7 Nov. 1855.

Disraeli accepting again in 1860 that 'the cards will play into our hands if we are quiet'.[49] Quiescence was not the product of apathy, but astute calculation.

In pursuing this opposition strategy Derby also devoted time and energy to the management of Conservative votes in the Commons. Over parliamentary reform, in October 1851, Derby pronounced that 'my idea is that we should abstain from pledging ourselves to resist any and every measure which may be brought forward, at the same time that we deprecate the introduction of any extensive alteration as uncalled for by any necessity or strong public feeling'.[50] At the height of the sectarian furore excited by Russell's 'Durham Letter' in December 1850, Derby was content rather to 'follow the stream which is running quite strong enough, than attempt to take a lead of our own. I think the government are in an awkward dilemma ... and the more rope we give them the more chance there is of their hanging themselves at one or the other.'[51] As Derby summarized this opposition strategy to Disraeli in January 1853: 'we must to a certain extent keep up the spirits of our party; but we must exercise, and get them to exercise, great patience and forbearance, if we do not wish, by an active and bitter opposition, to consolidate the present combination between those who have no real bond of union, and who must, I think, fall to pieces before long, if left to themselves'.[52] This was 'killing with kindness'.[53] Derby's abiding dictum was, 'wait, don't attack ministers, that will only bind them together. If let alone they must fall to pieces by their own disunion.'[54] On the three occasions he came to power, in 1852, 1858 and 1866, it was because of differences within non-Conservative opinion, not Conservative offensives. In 1852 Palmerston attacked Russell, in 1858 Russell and the radicals attacked Palmerston, and in 1866 the Adullamites attacked Russell and Gladstone. This was confirmation of the intelligence of Derby's strategy of 'armed neutality'.[55]

This strategic passivity was not indifference, indolence or a confession of doctrinal bankruptcy. Derby involved himself constantly in the management and preservation of party support in the Commons. Certainly he engaged himself in the affairs of the Commons party more directly and consistently than Salisbury deigned to do in the 1880s and 1890s. As Derby assured Lord Lonsdale in December 1853, he wished to have his party 'well in hand'.[56] In this regard Derby's efforts were decidedly successful. He often communicated directly with the Commons whips. First of all with William Beresford and Charles Newdegate, and after 1853 he conferred even more closely with the astute and popular Sir William Jolliffe. Indeed, Jolliffe made it a prior condition to his becoming chief whip that the backbenches clearly understood that he was Derby's, not just Disraeli's, choice. If he was seen as Disraeli's appointment, Jolliffe warned Derby, 'I should not retain the post a moment.'[57] Such was Derby's

---

[49] Disraeli to Derby, 27 May 1860, cited in Monypenny and Buckle, *Disraeli*, IV, 273.
[50] Derby to Disraeli, 26 Oct. 1851, cited in *ibid.*, III, 331–2.
[51] Derby to Malmesbury, 2 Dec. 1850, cited in Malmesbury, *Memoirs*, I, 267.
[52] Derby to Disraeli, 30 Jan. 1853, cited in Monypenny and Buckle, *Disraeli*, III, 483.
[53] *Disraeli, Derby and the Conservative Party*, ed. Vincent, p. 92.
[54] *Ibid.*, p. 94.
[55] Derby MSS 920 DER(14) 182/1: Derby to Walpole, 30 Jan. 1853.
[56] *Ibid.*, 182/2: Derby to Lonsdale, 20 Dec. 1853.
[57] *Ibid.*, 158/10: Jolliffe to Derby, 18 Aug. 1853.

close contact with the Commons whips that, in 1847, Lord George Bentinck stepped down as protectionist leader in the Commons complaining of Derby's direct communications with Beresford and Newdegate.[58] This direct consultation, Bentinck protested, undermined his own authority and made his continued leadership of the Commons party untenable. Bentinck's protest, however, did not dissuade Derby from maintaining close and confidential relations with the Commons whips.

In January 1857 Jolliffe observed to Derby that 'whenever a peer shall be leader of a political party, a somewhat divided leadership in the House of Commons will naturally result'.[59] The leadership of the Commons party was a recurrent difficulty. The mercurial Bentinck was a volatile, passionate and unreliable lieutenant who, between 1846 and 1848, repeatedly alienated sections of his own backbenches. A period of uneasy and unstable arrangements followed, involving the wavering Lord Granby, the superannuated John Herries, and the widely mistrusted Disraeli. Not until 1850 was Disraeli eventually recognised by Derby as sole leader of the Conservatives in the Commons. After 1850, despite his own well-founded suspicions, Derby tried to bolster Disraeli's authority amongst Conservative M.P.s. In 1854 Derby insisted on Disraeli giving an eve-of-session dinner. At Derby's suggestion, for the first time, Disraeli also hosted a full gathering of the Commons party at his own London residence in Grosvenor Gate. This was part of Derby's campaign to ensure that Disraeli had 'more frequent intercourse' with the Conservative backbenches.[60] During the 1854 session Derby urged Disraeli to meet Conservative M.P.s each Saturday afternoon at Grosvenor Gate; this regular consultation securing 'a concurrence of opinion and a uniformity of action'.[61] These meetings continued during the 1855 session, but lapsed in 1856. 'Much of the disorganisation which has prevailed', Derby commented to Jolliffe, 'has been owing to the want of unrestricted intercourse of this kind.' There was much, Derby declared, 'that *must* be managed by the leader of the Commons'.[62] At a large party meeting on 30 January 1854, hosted by Derby in his own London residence in St James's Square, the Conservative leader 'eulogised Disraeli, who might have made mistakes, dropped expressions which would have been better unuttered, but whose ability and devotion to their interests could not be doubted'.[63] As a result, by the 1860s, Disraeli's position was becoming more secure, although persistent doubts about his commitment to Conservative principles remained. As the acerbic tory critic of Disraeli's leadership, Lord Robert Cecil, commented, there endured a suspicion that Disraeli's Conservative principles were an accident of his career.

Crises in Derby's relations with Disraeli were usually prompted by Disraeli's covert disregard for Derby's preferences. Disraeli's reckless pursuit of impractical alliances and idiosyncratic policies always brought swift reprimands from Derby, who had frequently to upbraid Disraeli for fermenting debilitating divisions within the Commons party. Against Derby's expressed wishes, during 1853 Disraeli entered

---

[58] *Ibid.*, 132/13: Bentinck to Derby, 24 Dec. 1847.
[59] *Ibid.*, 158/10: Jolliffe to Derby, 3 Jan. 1857.
[60] Hylton MSS DD/HY/18/1: Derby to Jolliffe, 6 Jan. 1854.
[61] Derby MSS 920 DER(14) 158/10: Jolliffe to Derby, 3 Jan. 1854.
[62] Hylton MSS DD/HY/18/1: Derby to Jolliffe, 6 Jan. 1854.
[63] *Disraeli, Derby and the Conservative Party*, ed. Vincent, p. 118.

into secret communications with the Irish brigade and the English radicals. Contrary to Derby's consistent request not to encourage popular anti-catholicism amongst Conservative supporters, thereby making sectarian differences the basis of party distinctions, during late 1853 Disraeli attempted to intensify protestant antipathy to Puseyite Peelites in government. Through his journalistic mouthpiece *The Press*, which denounced 'Jesuits in the guise of financiers' and 'impassioned Oratorians in the garb of Secretaries of War', Disraeli sought to fashion popular anti-tractarianism into a weapon against Peelite ministers.[64] In response Derby immediately decried the 'extreme pretensions' of the ultra-protestants, who were to be discouraged 'by the negative means of avoiding in debate, or in meetings of the party, language which may unnecessarily *frossier* their ... views'.[65] Even more forcefully, in October 1855, Derby decisively quashed Disraeli's championing of a Conservative peace initiative, opposing continuation of the Crimean war. In a fierce rebuke an infuriated Derby rejected such a policy as contrary to honour and their party's interests; the proposal outraging Conservative M.P.s by breeding rumours of a junction between Disraeli, Gladstone and John Bright.[66] Once again Disraeli was brought forcefully to heel. Derby's exasperation and anger was the more intense because of his persistent public attempts to assuage Conservative suspicions about Disraeli's real intentions; a rehabilitation all too often subverted by Disraeli's own unpredictable behaviour.

Derby's illness and depression, particularly during 1853 and 1856, could cause anxiety about his own leadership. 'The Captain's' seclusion, fragile health and evident despondency could cause even loyal figures, such as Jolliffe and Malmesbury, concern. But such apprehension never hardened into disloyalty. Anxiety produced pleas for Derby to act. What was sought were signs of Derby's continued willingness to lead. Moreover, Derby always responded to these pleas positively. Reacting to urging to act in January 1854 and January 1857, Derby hosted dinners for Conservative peers, addressed large party meetings at St James's Square, and reassured his followers through letters and conversation of his firm resolve. In 'great force' by January 1854, for example, Derby delivered a scathing critique in the Lords of the Aberdeen coalition's muddled foreign policy.[67] Likewise, in January 1857 Derby was once again 'in high force' and 'set the wheels agoing'; marshalling Conservatives for the imminent collapse of the Palmerston administration.[68] The Conservative parliamentary party, in turn, consistently responded to Derby's reaffirmations of leadership with enthusiastic expressions of support. Even the hostile diarist Charles Greville, clerk to the privy council, noted the 'striking fact' in February 1857 that the Conservative opposition, 'of whose disunion we have heard so much, and of the internal repulsion supposed to prevail among them, seems to be as united as ever'.[69] During the 1850s and 1860s very few Conservative M.P.s renounced the party whip. In July 1858 Malmesbury

---

[64] *The Press*, 24 Dec. 1853.

[65] Derby MSS 920 DER(14) 182/1: Derby to Disraeli, 14 Nov. 1853.

[66] Derby to Disraeli, 25 Oct. 1855, cited in Monypenny and Buckle, *Disraeli*, IV, 20.

[67] Bodleian Library, Hughenden MSS B/XX/HS/44: Malmesbury to Disraeli, 21 Jan. 1854, and Derby, 31 Jan. 1854; Hansard, *Parl. Debs*, 3rd ser., CXXX, 65–86.

[68] Hughenden MSS B/XX/J/43: Jolliffe to Disraeli, 29 Jan. 1857, and *ibid.*, B/XX/J/40: Jolliffe to Disraeli, 27 Dec. 1856.

[69] C. C. F. Greville, *The Greville Memoirs*, ed. Henry Reeve (8 vols, 1888), VIII, 85.

observed that Conservative M.P.s were now 'better disciplined than ... even in Peel's time'.[70] Lord Robert Cecil too noted in the *Quarterly Review* in October 1867 that over the previous 20 years the Conservative party had 'become famous for its organisation and prompt discipline'.[71] Derby's Conservatives remained the largest single cohesive body of votes in the mid-Victorian Commons, despite Disraeli's unpredictability and unpopularity. Indeed, Disraeli usually provided a convenient target for those frustrations created by Derby's deliberate inactivity in opposition. Conservatives found it easier to distrust Disraeli than be disloyal to Derby.

Passivity in opposition was complemented by Derby's moderation in office. As prime minister in 1852, 1858–9 and 1866–8 Derby headed governments with a minority of support in the Commons. But his ministerial policies were more than the shifts and compromises demanded by the exigencies of minority government. As Derby informed the Lords in March 1858, 'there can be no greater mistake than to suppose that a Conservative ministry necessarily means a stationary ministry'. Rather, his government embraced responsible and considered progress, 'improving the old system, adapting our institutions to the purposes which they are intended to serve, and by judicious changes meeting the increased demands of society'.[72] Moderate reform was the keynote of Derby's policies in office. He refused to be 'a mere stop gap until it would suit the convenience of the Liberal party to forget their dissensions'. He wished to 'convert, if possible, an existing minority into a practical majority'.[73] As in opposition, so conventional expressions of patrician detachment from personal ambition belied a firm commitment to party success. Derby's surrender of the royal commission to form governments in 1851 and 1855 was not, as often suggested, evidence of his lack of political purpose. Rather, it was a determination to possess power on terms other than sufferance that informed his actions. 'It is a bungling fisherman who strikes at the first nibble', he advised his son. 'I shall wait until the fish has gorged the bait, and then I am sure to land him.'[74]

Despite his remoteness in the Lords Derby took an active interest in electoral matters as part of his engagement with party management. Where they occurred, constituency contests in mid-Victorian Britain were largely the product of local circumstances; what one long-serving Conservative M.P. described to Jolliffe as the 'wheels within wheels'.[75] The Westminster leadership had a limited influence in constituency affairs, local partisans often resenting outside interference. Derby publicly endorsed what he saw as the legitimate influence of local landowners in constituency matters. His own experience of popular electoral contests as a young M.P., in Preston in 1830 for instance, reinforced his prejudices against the susceptibility of voters exposed to dangerous demagogues and contemptuous of local landed *élites*. Patronage, as the lubricant of party connexion, provided an invaluable means of rewarding loyal efforts and reinforcing local landed influence, and in these matters Derby took a

---

[70] Hughenden MSS B/XX/HS/67: Malmesbury to Disraeli, 6 July 1858.

[71] *Lord Salisbury on Politics. A Selection from his Articles in the Quarterly Review, 1860–1883*, ed. Paul Smith (Cambridge, 1972), p. 285.

[72] Derby, 1 Mar. 1858, Hansard, *Parl. Debs*, 3rd ser., CXLIX, 41.

[73] See Jones *Lord Derby and Victorian Conservatism*, p. 318.

[74] *Disraeli, Derby and the Conservative Party*, ed. Vincent, p. 44.

[75] Hylton MSS DD/HY/19/81: Burroughes to Jolliffe, 26 May [1858].

close interest. In 1854, for example, Derby recommended Lord Portarlington for a vacancy in the Irish representative peerage for his exertions in securing a Conservative electoral victory in the Irish borough of Portarlington and as a guarantee of his support at the next election. Three years later, in 1857, Portarlington contributed £100 to the Conservative election fund.[76] Thus Derby sought to sway, even if he could not control, constituency contests.

In 1853 Conservative electoral management was vested in the hands of Disraeli's solicitor Philip Rose, aided by Markham Spofforth as party agent. Together with Jolliffe, Rose and Spofforth undertook the repair of Conservative constituency organization. Prior to 1846, under the direction of Francis Bonham, the fostering of Conservative associations in the constituencies had assumed an unprecedented efficiency. But during the late 1840s neither Bentinck nor Disraeli took a close interest in electoral affairs. To the discomfort of Derby this left a void partially filled by militant protectionist associations. In 1852 Beresford's inept attempts to galvanise Conservative electoral feeling led to damming accusations of corruption and bribery. After 1853 Jolliffe, Rose and Spofforth looked to restore the vitality and legitimacy of Conservative constituency organization. This was an undertaking of which Derby heartily approved. In December 1856, as part of his rallying of Conservatives in Westminster, Derby contributed to the party electoral fund.[77] From the Carlton Club these funds were then judiciously distributed to assist in electoral expenses. Derby again contributed personally to the fund in 1859.

As well as supporting financially loyal M.P.s, Derby also, on occasion, took steps to influence electoral contests where more wayward Conservatives were standing. In March 1857, for example, Derby dedicated considerable effort to attempting to defeat 'Ben' Bentinck's candidature in West Norfolk. Although nominally a Conservative, during the 1852–7 parliament Bentinck had repeatedly voted with the government and consistently tried to undermine Disraeli's authority as Commons leader. Alarmed at reports that the loyal Conservative William Bagge was going to give way to Bentinck's nomination in the forthcoming general election, Derby immediately wrote in March 1857 to the Norfolk landowner Lord Sondes condemning Bentinck's conduct as 'wholly inconsistent with the ordinary obligations of party'.[78] As well as providing proof of Derby's active interest in electoral matters, however, the episode also reveals the limited influence party leaders exercised over constituency affairs. In the event the views of local magnates prevailed. Bentinck was returned as one of the two M.P.s for the county constituency in an uncontested election. In a similar fashion, in 1863 Derby attempted to put local pressure on the recently elected Liberal-Conservative John Peel, M.P. for Tamworth. Considering Peel 'a very slippery gentleman', Derby suggested to Disraeli that the whips could 'give a hint to his Tamworth friends to put the screw on him'.[79] Though forced to work with

---

[76] *Ibid.*, DD/HY/18/8: Eglinton to Jolliffe, 20 Mar. 1857. See Stewart *Foundation of the Conservative Party*, p. 326.

[77] Derby contributed £1,000, as did Lords Lonsdale and Salisbury. Other contributions raised the total to between £7–8,000. West Sussex R.O., Richmond MSS 1800/357: Derby to Richmond, 7 Mar. 1857. See Hogan 'Party Management in the Lords', p. 135.

[78] Derby MSS 920 DER(14) 183/2: Derby to Sondes, 14 Mar. 1857.

[79] Hughenden MSS B/XX/S/316: Derby to Disraeli, 19 Nov. 1863.

the grain of local feeling, Derby was none the less quite prepared to smooth the way for loyal supporters and encourage constituency resistance to renegade M.P.s. In 1864 Derby supported Taylor and Spofforth's establishment of the Junior Carlton Club, which brought together local notables, such as solicitors, upon whom Conservative constituency organization much depended.[80] The efficiency of Bonham's regime was never quite restored under Derby. But when the need or opportunity arose Derby was prepared to use his influence to work in assisting the effectiveness of popular Conservative support.

The conventional portrait of Derby as an apathetic aristocrat, indifferent to political success, has confused manner with motivation. Appearances belied a genuine commitment to party advantage. Inactivity was not indolence, nor was a pose of detachment, in reality, indifference. Working within the idiom and structures of mid-Victorian parliamentary government Derby maintained an active engagement with party management in the Lords, the Commons and outside Westminster. Difficulties with Disraeli, illness and depression often hampered his efforts. The militancy of protectionist associations and anti-catholic organizations often threatened to embarrass his careful policy pronouncements. Derby also generally regarded the press with wariness. Unlike Palmerston he never cultivated journalistic support to compensate for parliamentary weaknesses. Despite the expansion of newspapers in the 1850s, Malmesbury noted that 'Derby has never been able to realise the sudden growth and power of the political press, for which he has no partiality, which feeling is reciprocated by its members.'[81] Derby, Gladstone observed, was too much of a parliamentary politician to seek the 'strength of public opinion'.[82] Yet, despite his limitations, Derby was, as a party leader, fully committed to the management of his parliamentary support. In private conversation in January 1854 Disraeli suggested that the house of lords was the weakness of the aristocracy. It possessed privileges on condition of never using them. 'Put the territorialists into the Commons', he speculated, 'and what influence they would have.'[83] By more subtle means Derby successfully exercised, throughout his leadership from 1846 to 1868, a profound influence on the Conservative party, demonstrating the continued power of aristocratic leadership in mid-Victorian politics.

---

[80] Derby MSS 920 DER(14) 146/1: Disraeli to Derby, 14 Aug. 1863. See Gurowich, 'Party and Independence.' pp. 281–2.

[81] Malmesbury, *Memoirs*, II, 73.

[82] Gladstone memo., 6 Mar. 1857, B.L., Add. MS 44655, f. 62, cited in *The Gladstone Diaries* ed. M. R. D. Foot and H. C. G. Matthews, (14 vols, Oxford, 1968–94), V, 203. Although, interestingly, Derby approved the offering of a secret loan to the proprietor of two tory daily papers, the *Morning Herald* and the *Standard*, in February 1858 to rescue them from closure. See Hughenden MSS B/XX/R/8: Rose to Disraeli, 19 Feb. 1858.

[83] *Disraeli, Derby and the Conservative Party*, ed. Vincent, p. 117.

Salisbury's Definition of the Powers of the Lords

PETER MARSH

No statesman upset liberal expectations of progress more effectively than the third marquess of Salisbury. And in no arena was this achievement more evident than in his leadership of the house of lords. Reversing the almost universal assumption after the passage of the 1832 Reform Act that the influence of the upper House would diminish, Salisbury lifted its constitutional powers in the final two decades of the century to a height unprecedented during its course.[1] He nevertheless refused the pleas of his Radical Unionist ally Joseph Chamberlain to invest the house of lords with still further powers of legislative initiative. Salisbury's achievement was in every sense conservative. He wished to reinvigorate rather than to extend the traditional powers of the Lords. He hoped to use those powers to retard the erosion of the existing social, economic and religious order of Great Britain rather than to erect new fortifications adapted to the changing industrial and competitive imperial order such as Chamberlain wanted to construct.[2] Salisbury possessed the rare ability and he also enjoyed the rare good fortune to achieve what he sought and to avoid what he did not desire: but only for his own day.

His heightening of the role played by the house of lords in British political practice began in the spring of 1868 when he acceded to the peerage on the death of his father and had to surrender his seat in the Commons. Admirers of his unyielding brand of Conservatism were dismayed at his prospective removal from the currently stronger House, and they urged him to make an unprecedented attempt to refuse to inherit the title. He considered doing so, taking advantage of some difficulty in finding the register of his father's marriage. But he was 'so disgusted with the course the Tories had pursued in respect of Dizzy's Reform Bill that [he] did not think it worth the trouble to stay in the House of Commons'.[3] The dexterity of Disraeli and the alacrity of the Conservatives in the Commons in agreeing in 1867 to enfranchise the urban working class after throwing out a more moderate Liberal measure to the same effect infuriated Salisbury at the demoralization of the party and its surrender of the most effective barrier against the onrush of democracy. The Reform Act led Salisbury to try to strengthen the remaining barriers including the house of lords and accentuated his critique of the electoral pretensions upon which the house of commons based its

---

[1] The most perceptive analysis of this accomplishment is Corinne Comstock's 'Salisbury and the Lords, 1868–1895', in *Peers, Politics and Power. The House of Lords, 1603–1911*, ed. Clyve Jones and David Lewis Jones (1986), pp. 461–87.

[2] My argument here is in sharp contrast to that of David Steele in his able biography of *Lord Salisbury* (1999).

[3] Salisbury to Lord Wolmer, 7 Feb. 1893, in P. T. Marsh, *The Discipline of Popular Government. Lord Salisbury's Domestic Statecraft, 1881–1902* (Hassocks, Sussex, 1978), p. 4.

claim to pre-eminence. Accordingly from the time he entered the house of lords, long before he became its leader, he asserted its right to parity with the house of commons as a way to advance his particular conservative agenda. A strengthened upper House would not merely minimise his individual loss of influence on departure from the Commons but help the propertied aristocracy collectively to rival the claim of the lower House to interpret the wishes of the nation.

This agenda came into play as soon as Salisbury entered the Lords. Gladstone had just regrouped the Liberal forces in the Commons after their setback the previous year by attacking the most glaring of Ireland's grievances, the establishment and endowment of the sister church to the Church of England as the Church of Ireland though only a small minority of the Irish population belonged to it. A bill that Gladstone introduced to suspend new appointments to the Church of Ireland for a year during which a new general election was bound to occur swept through the house of commons up to the Lords. Salisbury used the occasion to raise the position of the assembly to which he now belonged by enunciating what has rightly been called 'the daring proposition that on a given occasion the house of lords might be more representative of public opinion than the house of commons'.[4] He drew a sharp distinction between the will of a current majority in the house of commons and an unmistakable expression of the will of the nation. While the house of lords, whatever its own inclination, would have to yield to the latter, it need show no such subservience to the former.

The general election that took place at the end of the year revolved around the issue of Irish disestablishment, and Gladstone won a large majority in its favour. The bill that Gladstone promptly introduced in the new parliament won ready assent in the Commons. But the response of the Lords remained very much in doubt after the Conservative peers at the urging of the former prime minister, Lord Derby, decided to vote against the measure. Salisbury, gripped by revulsion at the memory of the 1867 Reform Act, diverged with increasing determination from this proposed course of action. Derby had been prime minister when the Reform Act passed, and he was seconded in his opposition to the Irish Church bill by Lord Cairns, Disraeli's lieutenant in the upper House. Principle as well as personalities drove Salisbury in the opposite direction. He had been sickened in 1867 by the readiness with which the Conservatives in parliament abandoned their repeated pronouncements against extension of the franchise and embraced it when it would advance their party fortunes. In 1868 the Conservative peers, Cairns even more emphatically than Salisbury, had justified their rejection of Gladstone's suspensory bill for appointments to the Irish Church by appealing beyond the house of commons to the verdict of the forthcoming general election. That verdict was now in, clear and emphatic. Salisbury insisted on accepting it. He even voted for the Irish Church Bill, much though he loathed it, when its defeat appeared otherwise likely. But he accompanied his action by repeating with emphatic clarity his insistence on the complete equality of the two houses of parliament. They were subject, he insisted, not to each other but only to the clearly expressed will of the nation. Salisbury acted accordingly during the subsequent debate over amendments to the bill when he pressed for greater concessions from the

---

[4] Comstock Weston, 'Salisbury and the Lords', p. 467.

Salisbury's Definition 93

The Home Rule Debate in the House of Lords, 9 September 1893. By Dickinson and Foster. By permission of the Parliamentary Estates Directorate, Palace of Westminster.

government than Gladstone was willing to make or that Disraeli in the Commons and his allies in the Lords were willing to insist upon.[5]

There was no need for further development in Salisbury's constitutional doctrine over the next ten years, particularly after the Conservatives won the general election of 1874 and Salisbury and Disraeli learned to work together. But the heavy defeat of the Conservatives in the general election of 1880 reactivated the constitutional controversy. Salisbury issued a withering analysis of the electoral base that brought the Liberals back to power. Questioning the mandate that the Liberals claimed to have received from the electorate, he repeatedly pointed out that if 2,000 voters in the constituencies where the contest was closest had cast their ballots for Conservatives instead of Liberals, the Liberals would not have emerged with a majority in the house of commons.[6] At an abstract but fundamental level he also exposed the dubious assumptions underlying the claim of the house of commons generally to represent the electorate, let alone the people: the assumption

> for instance, that those present at the process of voting represent the absent; that a majority, however small, represents the whole; that a man's mind is a perfect reflex of the minds of fifty thousand of his fellow-citizens on all subjects because he was chosen, as the best of two or three candidates, in respect to a particular crisis and a particular set of subjects, by a bare majority of those who took the trouble to vote on a particular day.[7]

Salisbury's determination to elevate the house of lords to parity with the Commons as an interpreter of the will of the nation could not, however, have much practical effect until he brought the Conservative peerage to act accordingly. Though his conspicuous powers of intellect and argument commanded respect among the Conservative peers, his eagerness to lead them into battle against the Commons made them nervous, afraid of provoking a contest of 'the peers versus the people' which the peers were likely to lose. This attitude, far from preserving the powers of the upper House against further erosion, was in fact weakening them through disuse. But Salisbury had yet to convince his fellow peers of this uncomfortable truth. They preferred to follow the less aggressive leadership of Disraeli's friends in the Lords – Cairns, the duke of Richmond, and the fifteenth earl of Derby, heir to the former prime minister – and then of Disraeli himself when he became earl of Beaconsfield. They would have preferred to bring Richmond back as leader in 1881 when Disraeli died,[8] but Richmond deferred to Salisbury in view of his obvious brilliance once Salisbury indicated his willingness to assume the lead.

His first two years as Conservative leader in the Lords were not encouraging. The Conservative peers proved unwilling either to reject outright the main Liberal measures sent up by the house of commons or to insist upon amendments to bills to

---

[5] Steele, *Lord Salisbury*, pp. 67–8.

[6] Salisbury, 'Ministerial Embarrassments', *Quarterly Review*, CLI (1881), 541; Salisbury to the South Essex Registration Association, *The Times*, 25 May 1882, p. 11c; Salisbury at Dorchester, *The Times*, 17 Jan. 1884, p. 10c.

[7] Salisbury, 'Disintegration', *Quarterly Review*, CLVI (1883), 571.

[8] Andrew Roberts, *Salisbury* (1999), p. 255.

which they had agreed in principle. Salisbury's attempts to induce the Conservative peers to abide by the threats and pledges they made in the early stages of legislative debate proved counterproductive. His efforts publicly exposed the division in strategy between his hard line and the moderation of Cairns and Richmond publicly and, still more seriously, demonstrated that a substantial majority of the Conservative lords sided with the moderates. Salisbury had to admit after the second of these setbacks, over the Irish Arrears Bill of 1882, that he had suffered 'a tremendous smash'.[9] 'Made to look reactionary and isolated in the most public way possible,' as Andrew Roberts observes in his recent biography, 'Salisbury had reached the nadir of his leadership of the Tories in the Lords, indeed of his whole post-1867 career.'[10]

This smash was in line with the progressive expectation that sooner or later all attempts to arrest the tide toward democracy were doomed to fail. In his pessimistic mode Salisbury resigned himself to such a future. But he had another side, he was also a fighter. And the remarkable thing about Salisbury's achievement in politics was that the fighter prevailed. Just two years after his humiliation over the Arrears Bill, he managed to turn the passage of the Reform Bill into a spectacular vindication of his strategy for the house of lords.

The achievement was riddled with irony. It occurred together with the most radical transformation of the electorate in the whole of the nineteenth century; and Salisbury was personally responsible for the most radical aspect of that transformation, the creation almost everywhere in the country of equal electoral districts. This behaviour struck some of his right-wing friends and left-wing enemies as inexplicable. How could it be squared with his furious repudiation of Disraeli over the Second Reform Act? Furthermore, the outcome of the agitation over the Reform Bill in 1884[11] was not what he set out to achieve. What he most wanted was to force the government to call a general election on the existing basis as prescribed in the 1867 act, and he conveyed the impression that he might be willing to sacrifice the house of lords to attain this end. The ways in which he strengthened the house of lords and brought out the Conservative inclinations of the expanding suburbs were tactical by-products, secondary fruits of his strategy.

The turnaround in his fortunes had a dual origin. It owed much to the tactical skill he had developed during his first difficult years as leader. But it depended equally on the realization among the peers who had produced those difficulties that Salisbury's fears of Gladstone's approach to electoral reform were well founded. The bill that Gladstone introduced in the spring of 1884 would give the franchise to householders in county constituencies without any redrawing of constituency boundaries to deal with the resulting inequities in electoral size. Almost all the Conservative leaders including Cairns and Richmond agreed with Salisbury that such a measure would destroy the electoral base of their party for a generation. They therefore fully endorsed Salisbury's proposal to meet the Franchise Bill when it went up to the Lords with a

---

[9] Quoted in Steele, *Lord Salisbury*, p. 169.

[10] Roberts, *Salisbury*, p. 271.

[11] The best monographic study of this agitation is still Andrew Jones's *The Politics of Reform 1884* (Cambridge, 1972). There is an excellent account from Salisbury's standpoint in chapter 18 of Andrew Roberts' biography.

reasoned amendment refusing to pass the measure until it was accompanied with a redistribution of seats or redrawing of constituency boundaries.

There was still plenty of room for disagreement within the Conservative consensus; and Gladstone endeavoured to break it apart. He did so by fomenting a popular 'peers against the people' agitation to play upon the fears of the timid members of the upper House rather than address the substantive issue of redistribution that worried Cairns and Richmond. Salisbury responded with a subtler mixture of tactics. In the first place, redistribution had as much to do with electoral representation of the people as did widening the franchise. In focussing on redistribution, Salisbury blunted the ability of the Liberals to respond to his challenge as a matter of principle. He countered the public demonstrations that the Liberals organized against the peers by mobilizing Conservative demonstrations on the other side. Though the Conservative demonstrations did not equal the Liberal ones in size, at least they showed that 'the people' were by no means all on one side. He also addressed the subject of redistribution in 'A Note on Electoral Statistics' published by the *National Review* to indicate that he took it seriously and was willing to consider a wide range of unprecedented devices to ensure that propertied and educated minorities were not overwhelmed by simple majorities. These tactics did not eliminate the risk that Conservative peers like Cairns and Richmond would cave in under the pressure of the mass campaign that the Liberals kept up for several months. Salisbury used his position as the official leader of the Conservatives in the Lords to supervise the private negotiations that went on out of public view between peace seekers on both sides. Still he braced himself for yet another failure, a conclusive one this time that might well induce him to abandon the fight and resign the leadership in the Lords.

He was as much astonished as delighted when Gladstone and the Liberals caved in before the week-kneed tory peers did. The leaders on both sides convened in private conclave at Salisbury's Arlington Street house in London. The two of them most familiar with the detail of redistribution, Sir Charles Dilke on the Liberal side and Salisbury on the tory, hammered out the detail of a bill to be enacted immediately after the acceptance of the Franchise Bill by the house of lords. By holding out longer than the Liberal majority in the Commons, the Conservative majority in the Lords thus strengthened its constitutional claims although the stiffness of its spine depended largely on Salisbury's steel.

Though the upper House had successfully asserted its right to hold back a major piece of legislation until its wishes were met, this achievement did not yet amount to parity with the house of commons. To reach parity, to be able to speak for the nation with as much credibility as the elected Commons could claim, the house of lords needed to acquire some kind of popular mandate. Salisbury found a mandate well suited to his purposes in the wake of the crisis that Gladstone precipitated over home rule for Ireland. The great value of Gladstone's proposal from Salisbury's point of view was its power of repulsion. It repelled both the house of lords and the British electorate and thus brought them more closely into line with each other. But because home rule repelled the former much more strongly and clearly than the latter, considerable ingenuity and skill would be required to establish any working consensus between the peers and the British people.

The impact of home rule was most evident in the Lords. It drove most of the aristocratic whigs out of the Liberal party into an alliance, the Unionist alliance, with the Conservatives to uphold the union with Ireland. In this way Gladstone's proposals extended Salisbury's control right across the upper House and also stiffened its instinct for resistance. At the same time though to a lesser extent, home rule disconcerted and disappointed a good many of the English and Scottish voters who had supported the Liberals in the general election that took place at the end of 1885 following the enactment of the Franchise and Redistribution Bills. The returns from that election and the one that Gladstone precipitated six months later over home rule suggested that the new electors in county constituencies expected a Liberal government to address their economic and social concerns close to home and were disappointed when Gladstone turned his attention instead to Ireland. While some voters changed allegiance between the two elections, the marked fall in turnout in the 1886 election and the failure of the Conservatives to win a Commons majority on their own indicated that many formerly Liberal voters now preferred to stay at home. There may have been more indifference than hostility to the Irish among the voters of England, Wales and Scotland, but there was little evidence of the union of hearts and minds that Gladstone sought to cultivate.

The electoral evidence indicated, in other words, that the inclination of the British people was not to endorse the next great measure of constitutional reform that Gladstone persisted in placing at the forefront of the political agenda. So long as the people remained in that frame of mind, the peers could validly claim to speak for the nation on this central issue regardless of what happened in the Commons. The situation gave the Lords exactly the kind of mandate Salisbury wanted for it, a mandate to reject Gladstonian home rule. The mandate was essentially negative. It might be extended to any subordinate part of the Liberal agenda. But it did not give the Lords any power of initiative. Salisbury did not relish any extension of the Lords' capacities beyond the power of resistance. His objectives remained profoundly conservative. Constructive or reforming measures were more likely to upset vested interests than to allay discontent, or so at least Salisbury argued against the progressive sections of his party and the Unionist alliance.

Salisbury's responsibilities as leader of the Lords were rarely a worry for him during the long remainder of his career. His sharpest critics in the upper House such as the earl of Derby were now subordinate allies in the fight against home rule, while the leaders of the opposition in the Lords such as Rosebery were more admiring than critical of Salisbury. When disagreements bubbled up during the interlude of Liberal government in the early 1890s between the Conservative peers and their Liberal Unionist allies led by the duke of Devonshire, Salisbury insisted on the Conservative course and readily prevailed.

Indeed this Liberal interlude brought Salisbury along with the house of lords to the height of their conjoint power. The general election of 1892 that brought the Liberals back into office had also borne out all that Salisbury claimed for the house of lords. For the majority that the Liberals won in the house of commons was small and completely dependent on continuing support from the contingent of Nationalist M.P.s elected in Ireland. In both England and Scotland the number of successful Unionist candidates solidly exceeded the number of Liberals. Patently the British people – that is to say the Scots and the English[12] – had come down once again against home rule. Their opinion was therefore better reflected by the house of lords than by the motley majority for home rule in the house of commons. Thus paradoxically the narrow Liberal and Nationalist victory in the house of commons validated Salisbury's claims of parity for the house of lords.

He saw to it that the Unionists in the Commons dealt with the Home Rule Bill that Gladstone duly introduced in such a way as to bear out his claims for the Lords. When the Unionist leaders in the two Houses met before the election to consider what they should do if the Liberals won and sent a Home Rule Bill from the lower to the upper House, Chamberlain suggested that the Lords pass it but with an accompanying amendment requiring a referendum to ensure that the electorate was consulted directly and specifically on the bill. Firmly Salisbury ruled that suggestion out.[13] After the disappointing results of the election from the Liberal standpoint became clear, Salisbury declared in the house of lords that 'in the year that is coming the centre of interest and the centre of action will be found within these walls'.[14] The Unionist leaders in the Commons and the Lords pursued complementary tactics to subject the Home Rule Bill that Gladstone duly introduced to its inevitable defeat. Chamberlain in the Commons exposed the bill to withering, protracted, clause-by-clause analysis with twofold intent. He probed, ultimately in vain, for points of difference to break up the alliance between the Liberals and Irish Nationalists and thus defeat the bill in the Commons. Salisbury paid little attention to the detailed substance of this debate. But he welcomed the other objective and dividend of Unionist obstruction in the Commons:[15] Gladstone had to resort to repeated closure and increasingly severe curtailment of debate to push his bill through, drastic measures that made a mockery of deliberations in the Commons and thus served to discredit the lower House *vis-à-vis* the house of lords.

Meanwhile Salisbury strove to maximise the anticipated opposition in the upper House and give it a truly national rather than partisan complexion. Tactfully he left to the archbishops rather than to the Conservative whip in the Lords the task of urging the bishops to cast their votes against the bill instead of abstaining on it. Along with Devonshire, Salisbury canvassed the 36 Liberal peers whose allegiance, whether to the Gladstonians or to the Unionists, was not yet clear. These efforts enjoyed total success. In the largest vote in the history of the house of lords, all the bishops, virtually all of the previously uncommitted Liberals, and even five of those reckoned to be loyal Gladstonians, joined the Unionists to throw the Home Rule Bill by a massive majority of more than ten to one. The people of London expressed their concurrence that night by cheering Salisbury through the streets as he made his way home.

Yet, in spite of this endorsement, Salisbury refused to press his claims for the house of lords further. He wanted it to remain a conservative institution, strong to resist but not to initiate proposals for change. After the defeat of the second

---

[12] Wales had gone with the Liberals.

[13] J. L. Garvin and Julian Amery, *The Life of Joseph Chamberlain* (6 vols, 1932–69), II, 577.

[14] Hansard, *Parl. Debs.*, 4th ser., VII, 58 (8 Aug. 1892).

[15] Corinne Comstock Weston makes much of this in her most recent work, *The House of Lords and Ideological Politics. Lord Salisbury's Referendal Theory and the Conservative Party, 1846–1922* (Philadelphia, 1995), ch. 5.

Home Rule Bill and Gladstone's retirement, Chamberlain approached Salisbury with an ambitious programme of legislative initiatives on social and economic concerns that the Unionist-controlled house of lords could flesh out as bills, not expecting their enactment by the Liberal and Nationalist majority in the Commons, but to woo swing voters whose allegiance at the next general election need no longer be determined by Irish issues. Salisbury responded coolly, but not for lack of sympathy with some of the proposals in Chamberlain's package. The Conservative leader was if anything more radical than the Radical Unionist on facilities to help working men buy their homes that figured in Chamberlain's programme; and Chamberlain included the subject of reduction of pauper immigration which Salisbury had already taken up. Generally, whereas Liberal and Labour proposals for social and economic reform accentuated lines of conflict between labour and capital, Chamberlain's programme sought cooperation. He and Salisbury had recently hammered out an agreement that promoted co-operation rather than class conflict in contrast to the Liberal scheme on the subject of workmen's compensation for industrial accidents. Salisbury rested his critique of Chamberlain's current package of proposals on the role that they envisaged for the house of lords and the underlying electoral rationale more than on the disturbance to propertied interests that might result. The function that best befitted the house of lords, its leader explained, was as 'a checking – not an originating – chamber'.[16] He also questioned Chamberlain's assumption that the outcome of elections depended more on swing voters than on the efforts of committed supporters who might be alienated by some of the proposed reforms.

Whichever of them was right, the massive triumph of their combined forces in general election of 1895 and their repetition of this triumph in the general election of 1900 disposed for a decade of any challenge to Salisbury's claim of parity for the house of lords with the house of commons. The Unionist peerage thus came to take it for granted, to regard the claim as recognized constitutional practice established during the 22 years when Salisbury led the upper House, the longest leadership that any one had held there, and arguably the most distinguished.

But the parity proved to be very short-lived. The house of lords extended and hence exploded the claims that Salisbury had made when it rejected the budget that the Liberal government backed by an enormous majority in the Commons in 1909 sent up to it. What course Salisbury, had he lived, would have taken on this occasion is not easy to guess. He had notably declined to resist, however much he disliked, the graduate death duties including increased assessment of the duty on land that the Liberals inaugurated in the budget of 1894. Only after the Lords had agreed to this measure did Salisbury make a statement objecting to the principle of graduated death duties, belittling the moral authority of the existing house of commons, and repudiating any implication that the Lords lacked the right to reject a finance bill.[17] Yet that parting statement gave his successors all the title they needed to follow the promptings of the spirit of defiance that he had instilled in them. The restraint with which he acted did not resonate down the years like the daring and seeming rashness of his rhetoric.

---

[16] Salisbury to Chamberlain, 9 Nov. 1894, quoted in Steele, *Lord Salisbury*, p. 281.

[17] Marsh, *The Discipline of Popular Government*, p. 233.

Index

Abbot, Charles, speaker of the house of commons 34, 35
Aberdeen, George Gordon, 4th earl [S] of 48, 52, 57, 58, 66, 76, 82, 83
Abingdon, Willoughby Bertie, 4th earl of 26
Acts:
    Corn Law (1840), repeal of 6, 7, 78
    Corporation (1661), repeal of 2
    Municipal Corporations (1835) 10
    Navigation (1661) 9, 83
    Parliament (1911) 44
    Quebec (1774), repeal of 26
    Reform (1832) 6, 76, 80
        (1867) 91, 92
        (1884) 95
    Stamp Act (1764), repeal of 16, 17
    Test (1672), repeal of 2
    Union with Ireland (1800) 36
Addington, Henry *see* Sidmouth, viscount
Albemarle, William Charles Keppel, 4th earl of 38, 62
Althorp, John Charles Spencer, styled viscount 1, 62–4
Anstey, Roger 40
Argyll, George Douglas Campbell, 7th duke [S] of 68
Armagh, archbishop of *see* Beresford, Lord John George
Asquith, Henry Herbert 2
Auckland, George Eden, 2nd baron 64, 65
    William Eden, 1st baron 31, 33, 34, 37, 41

Bagehot, Walter, *The English Constitution*, 76
Bagge, William 89
Balfour, Arthur 75
Bath, John Alexander Thynne, 4th marquess of 82
    Thomas Thynne, 2nd marquess of 4
Bathurst, Henry, 3rd earl 45, 46
Beaufort, Henry Somerset, 7th duke of 7
Bedford, John Russell, 6th duke of 62, 63
    Wriothesley Russell, 3rd duke of 18
Bellenden, John Ker, 5th lord [S] 36
Benson, Edward White, archbishop of Canterbury 98
Bentinck, George William Pierrepont, nicknamed 'Ben' 89
    Lord George 77, 86, 89
    William Henry Cavendish *see* Portland, duke of
Beresford, Lord John George, archbishop of Armagh 47
    William 85, 89
Bertie, Willoughby *see* Abingdon, earl of

Bessborough, John George Brabazon Ponsonby, 5th earl [I] of 67
Bills:
    Abolition of Paper Duty (1860) 9
    Abolition of Slavery (1789) 40
        (1799) 40, 41
        (1804) 40
        (1806) 40, 42
    Amendment of Parliamentary Oath (1858) 82
    Annuity and Lottery (1781) 25
    Army Reform (1806) 32
    Bank (1803) 38
    Census (1800) 34
    Corn (1827) 44
        (1842) 72
    Declaratory (1766) 16
    Dissenters' Relief (1772) 20
        (1773) 8
    East India Company Restraining and Regulation (1772) 19
        (1773) 20
    Ecclesiastical Courts (1850) 67
    Encumbered Estates (1849) 68
    Foreign Slave Trade (1806) 33, 41
    Franchise (1884) 95–7
    Irish Arrears (1882) 95
    Irish Charities 35
    Irish Church (1833) 5, 47, 50, 52
        (1868) 92
    Irish Corporations (1836) 51
    Irish Home Rule (1893) 10, 98
    Irish Municipal Corporations (1840) 66
    Irish Poor Relief (1847) 68, 69
    Irish Poor Law (1836) 5
        (1838) 5, 48
    Irish Tithe (1834) 5
        (1836) 8
    Jewish Emancipation (1834) 5
    Military Reforms (1871) 9
    Municipal Corporations (1835) 49
    New Shoreham (1771) 24
    Nullum Tempus (1769) 19
    Paper Duties (1860) 83
    Rates in Aid (1849) 71
    Redistribution (1884) 9, 97
    Reform (1780) 26
        (1831) 4, 43
        (1832) 6, 47
        (1849) 59
        (1851) 59, 66, 85
        (1852) 59
        (1853) 59, 68
        (1867) 91, 95
        (1884) 9, 10, 95

Bills: (*Continued*)
  Roman Catholic Oath (1865) 83
  Royal Marriages (1772) 24–5
  Suspending New Appointments in the Church of Ireland (1868) 92
  Tobacco (1789) 30
  University Admission (1834) 5
Blomefield, Charle James, bishop of London 67, 70
Bonham, Francis 89, 90
Boscawen, Edward *see* Falmouth, earl of
Bright, John 73, 87
Brougham, Henry, 1st baron 57, 59, 64, 65, 69, 70
Buccleuch, Walter Francis Montagu-Douglas-Scott, 5th duke [S] of 54
Buckingham, Richard Grenville, 2nd duke of 45, 62
Burdett, Sir Francis 62
Burke, Edmund 19, 28
  Thoughts on the Cause of Present Discontents 20
Byng, John *see* Strafford, earl of

Cairns, Hugh McCalmont, 1st baron 92, 94–5
Campbell, John, 1st baron, chancellor 66, 68, 78, 79
Canning, George 31, 57, 62
Canterbury, archbishop of *see* Benson, Edward White
Cardwell, Edward 9, 81
Carlisle, Frederick Howard, 5th earl of 61
Carnarvon, Henry John Herbert, 3rd earl of 50
Cavendish, Spencer Compton *see* Devonshire, 8th duke of,
  William George Spencer *see* Devonshire, 6th duke of
Cecil, James Brownlow William *see* Salisbury, 2nd marquess of
  Lord Robert *see* Salisbury, 3rd marquess of
  Robert Arthur Talbot *see* Salisbury, 3rd marquess of
Chamberlain, Joseph 91, 98, 99
  Neville 75
Chatham, William Pitt, 1st earl 16, 18, 21, 24
Chichester, Thomas Pelham, 1st earl of 37, 38
Clarence, duke of *see* William IV, king
Clarendon, George William Frederick Villiers, 4th earl of 58, 64, 66–8, 70
Cobden, Richard 73
Copley, John Singleton *see* Lyndhurst, baron
Cottenham, Charles Christopher Pepys, 1st earl of 67, 68
Cowper, William, 1st earl 28
Creevey, Thomas 63
Crofton, Edward, 2nd baron [I] 54
Cumberland, duke of *see* Ernest Augustus, prince

Danby, Thomas Osborne, earl of 15
Dartmouth, William Legge, 2nd earl of 25

Davis, Richard, professor 42
Dawson-Damer, Henry John Reuben *see* Portarlington, earl of
De Grey, George Frederick Samuel Robinson, 3rd earl 9
De la Warr, George John West, 5th earl 47
Derby, Edward Geoffrey Stanley, 14th earl of, previously 2nd Baron Stanley 1, 9–11, 44, 64, 68, 71–3, 75–90, 92
  father of 80
  son(s) of 77, 80
  Edward Henry Stanley, 15th earl of 77, 94
Desart, John Otway O'Connor, 3rd earl [I] of 82
De Vesci, John Vesey, 2nd viscount 53
  son of 53
Devonshire, Spencer Compton Cavendish, 8th duke of, previously styled marquess of Hartington 81, 97, 98
  William George Spencer Cavendish, 6th duke of 61
Dilke, Sir Charles 96
Disraeli, Benjamin 49, 50, 75, 77–9, 84–8, 90, 94
Ditchfield, Grayson 8, 27
Douglas, Sylvester *see* Glenbervie, baron
Dowdeswell, William 22
Dumont, Etienne 59
Dundas, Henry *see* Melville, 1st viscount
  Robert *see* Melville, 2nd viscount
Dunraven, Windham Henry Wyndham-Quin, 2nd earl [I] of 53
Durham, John George Lambton, 1st earl of 52

Ebrington, Hugh Fortescue, styled viscount 1, 62
Eden, George *see* Auckland, 2nd baron
  William *see* Auckland, 1st baron
Edward Augustus, prince, duke of York 61
Effingham, Thomas Howard, 3rd earl of 24
Eglinton, Archibald William Montgomerie, 13th earl [S] of 82
Eldon, John Scott, 1st earl of, previously baron, chancellor 37, 45, 46
Ellenborough, Edward Law, 1st baron 62
Ellice, Edward 70
Elliot-Murray-Kynynwood, William Hugh *see* Minto, earl of
Ernest Augustus, prince, duke of Cumberland 51
Erskine, James *see* Rosslyn, earl of
  Thomas, 1st baron, chancellor 39

Falmouth, Edward Boscawen, 1st earl of 50
Farnham, John Maxwell-Barry, 5th baron [I] 53
Farrell, Stephen 1, 11
Fitzgerald, William Vescy-Fitzgerald, 1st baron 51
Fitzroy, Augustus Henry *see* Grafton, duke of
Fitzwilliam, Richard, 7th viscount [I] 33, 38
Forster, W.E. 9
Fortescue, Hugh *see* Ebrington, viscount
Fox, Charles James 24, 32, 37, 39, 41, 57, 59

Henry Richard *see* Holland, baron
Freeman-Mitford, John Thomas *see* Redesdale, earl of
Freemantle, William Henry   62

Gash, Norman   7
Gates, Horatio, general   25
George, prince of Wales *see* George IV, king
George III, king   8, 15, 16, 21, 26, 30, 32, 34
George IV, king, previously prince of Wales   3, 5, 41, 45, 62, 63
Germain, Lord George   26
Gladstone, William Ewart   2, 9, 10, 81, 83–5, 87, 90, 95–8
Glenbervie, Sylvester Douglas, baron [I]   37, 38
Goderich, viscount *see* Ripon, earl of
Grafton, Augustus Henry Fitzroy, 3rd duke of   16
Graham, James Robert George   64
    Sir James   81
Granby, Charles Cecil John Manners, styled marquess of   86
Granville, Lord Granville Leveson-Gower, 1st earl   58, 68, 81–3
Grenville, William Wyndham, baron   1, 11, 18, 29–42, 59, 60
Greville, Charles   87
    George *see* Warwick, 2nd earl of
    Henry Richard *see* Warwick, 3rd earl of
Grey, Charles, 2nd earl   38, 39, 47, 57, 58, 60–4, 76, 81
    Henry, 3rd earl, previously styled Viscount Howick   63, 68, 69

Halevy, Elie   6,7
Harley, Robert *see* Oxford, earl of
Harriss, James *see* Malmesbury, 1st earl of
    James Howard *see* Malmesbury, 3rd earl of
Hartington, marquess of *see* Devonshire, 8th duke of
Hawkesbury, baron *see* Liverpool, earl of
Hawkins, Angus   9, 12, 65
Heath, Edward   75
Herbert, Henry John George *see* Carnarvon, earl of
    Sidney   81
Herries, J.C.   62, 86
Hewett, John   25
Hobart, Robert, lord   37, 38
Holland, Henry Richard Fox, 3rd baron   37, 48, 62, 63, 65
Horner, Francis   59
Howard, Frederick *see* Carlisle, earl of
    Thomas *see* Effingham, earl of
Howick, viscount *see* Grey, 3rd earl
Huskisson, William   78
Hutchinson, John Hely-Hutchinson, baron   31

Jeffrey, Francis   59
Jenkinson, Charles *see* Liverpool, 1st earl of
    Robert Banks *see* Liverpool, 2nd earl of
Jersey, George Villiers, 5th earl of   62

Joliffe, Sir William   85–9

Keppel, Augustus, admiral   21, 27
    William Charles *see* Albemarle, earl of
Ker, John *see* Bellenden, lord
Kilmuir, David Patrick Maxwell Fyfe, 1st earl of   75
King, Peter, 7th lord   38
Kinglake, A.W.   69
Kitson Clark, G.   51

Lamb, George   43
    William *see* Melbourne, viscount
Lambton, John George *see* Durham, earl of
Lansdowne, Henry Petty, 3rd marquess of   1, 2, 9–11, 57–73, 81, 82
Large, David   58
Lauderdale, James Maitland, 8th earl [S] of   54
Leeds, Thomas Osborne, 4th duke of   30
Legge, William *see* Dartmouth, earl of
Leicester, George Townshend, 1st earl of   41
Lennox, Charles *see* Richmond, 3rd and 5th dukes of
    Charles Henry *see* Richmond, 6th duke of
Limerick, Edmond Henry Percy, 1st earl [I] of   35, 37
Liverpool, Charles Jenkinson, 1st earl of, previoulsy Baron Hawkesbury   30, 31, 33, 37, 38, 41
    Robert Bankes Jenkinson, 2nd earl of   3, 12, 29, 44, 52, 54
Lloyd George, David   2, 5
London, bishop of *see* Blomefield, Charles James
Londonderry, Charles William Vane, 3rd marquess [I] of   46, 48
Lonsdale, William Lowther, 2nd earl of   85
Loughborough, Alexander Wedderburn, 1st baron, chancellor   31, 34, 37
Lowther, William *see* Lonsdale, earl of
Lyndhurst, John Singleton Copley, baron   6, 45, 49–51, 65
Lytton, Edward Bulwer   78

McCahill, Michael   1, 11
Maclagan, William Dalrymple, archbishop of York   98
Major, John   75
Malmesbury, James Harris, 1st earl of   31
    James Howard Harris, 3rd earl of   82, 84, 87, 90
Malthus, Thomas Robert   39
Mandler, Peter   64
Manners, Charles Cecil John Manners *see* Granby, marquess of
Mansfield, William Murray, 1st earl of   35
    William David Murray, 3rd earl of   49
Marsh, Peter   9
Matthew, Colin   9
Maxwell-Barry, John *see* Farnham, baron
Maxwell Fyfe, David Patrick *see* Kilmuir, earl of

Melbourne, William Lamb, viscount [I]   8, 49, 50, 57, 58, 61, 63, 77, 79
Melville, Henry Dundas, 1st viscount   30, 35, 36, 38
  Robert Dundas, 2nd visount   45, 54
Milles, George John *see* Sondes, baron
Minto, William Hugh Elliot-Murray-Kynynwood, 3rd earl of   81
Mitchell, Leslie   5, 8
Moira, Francis Rawdon-Hasting, 2nd earl of   36
Monck, Henry Stanley *see* Rathdowne, earl of
Montagu, John *see* Sandwich, earl of
Montagu-Douglas-Scott, Walter Francis *see* Buccleuch, duke of
Monteagle, Thomas Spring Rice, 1st baron   64, 65, 69, 70
Montgomerie, Archibald William *see* Eglinton, earl of
Murray, William *see* Mansfield, 1st earl of
  William David *see* Mansfield, 3rd earl of

Nassau de Zuylestein, William Henry *see* Rochford, earl of
Newcastle, Henry Pelham Pelham-Clinton, 4th duke of   4, 47–50
  Thomas Pelham-Holles, 1st duke of   1, 13, 15–17, 28, 29
Newdegate, Charles   85
Newspapers and Journals:
  Illustrated London News   78
  National Review   96
  The Press   87
  Quarterly Review   88
North, Frederick, styled lord   8

O'Connell, Daniel   63, 80
O'Connor, John Otway *see* Desart, earl of
O'Gorman, Frank   13
Osborne, Thomas *see* Danby, earl of
  Thomas *see* Leeds, 4th duke of
Oxford, Robert Harley, 1st earl of   15

Pakington, Sir John   84
Palmerston, Henry John Temple, 3rd viscount [I]   57–9, 64–6, 70–2, 81, 83–5, 90
Parke, Sir James   81, 82
Parry, Jonathan   57
Peel, John   98
  Sir Robert, 2nd baronet   3, 46, 48, 49, 52, 54, 75, 78
Pelhan, Thomas, 2nd baron *see* Chichester, earl of
Pelham-Clinton, Henry Pelham *see* Newcastle, 4th duke of
Pelham-Holles, Thomas *see* Newcastle, 1st duke of
Percy, Edmond Henry *see* Limerick, earl of
Petty, John *see* Shelburne, earl of
Petty, Henry *see* Lansdowne, marquess of
Pitt, William, the elder *see* Chatham, earl of
  the younger   29, 30, 32, 35, 37, 41, 53, 57
Pleydell-Bouverie, Jacob *see* Radnor, earl of

Ponsonby, John George Brabazon *see* Bessborough, earl of
Portarlington, Henry John Reuben Dawson-Damer, 3rd earl [I] of   89
Portland, William Henry Cavendish Bentinck, 3rd duke of   53
Powell, John   9, 10
Powerscourt, Mervyn Wingfield, 7th viscount [I]   83
Primrose, Archibald Philip *see* Roseberry, earl of

Radnor, Jacob Pleydell-Bouverie, 2nd earl of   33
Rathdowne, Henry Stanley Monck, earl [I] of   53, 54
Rawdon-Hastings, Francis *see* Moira, earl of
Redesdale, John Thomas Freeman-Mitford, earl of   46, 82
Richmond, Charles Henry Lennox, 6th duke of   94–6
  Charles Lennox, 3rd duke of   19, 21, 23, 25, 26, 28
  Charles Lennox, 5th duke of   64
Rigby, Richard   19
Ripon, Frederick John Robinson, 1st earl of, previously Viscount Goderich   44, 45, 58, 62, 64
Roberts, Andrew   95
Robinson, Frederick John *see* Ripon, earl of
  George Frederick Samuel *see* De Grey, earl
Rochford, William Henry Nassau de Zuylestein, 3rd earl of   25
Rockingham, Charles Watson-Wentworth, 2nd marquess of   1, 11, 13–29
Roden, Robert Jocelyn, 3rd earl [I] of   6, 53, 54
Rose, Philip   89
Roseberry, Archibald Philip Primrose, 5th earl [S] of   97
Rosslyn, James Erskine, 2nd earl of   62
Rothschild, Lionel de, baron   82
Russell, John *see* Bedford, 6th duke of
  Lord John   9, 51, 57–9, 62–8, 70–3, 82, 85
  Wriothesley *see* Bedford, 3rd duke of

Sainty, Sir John   1, 29, 59
Salisbury, James Brownlow William Cecil, 2nd marquess of   50
  Robert Arthur Talbot Cecil, 3rd marquess of, previously Lord Robert Cecil   1–3, 9–11, 85, 86, 88, 91–9
Sandwich, John Montagu, 4th earl of   19
Scott, John *see* Eldon, earl of
Sealy, Lovell   69
Shelburne, John Petty, earl [I] of   24–6, 59
Shore, John *see* Teignmouth, baron
Sidmouth, Henry Addington, 1st viscount, previously speaker of the house of commons   35, 37, 39, 41
Smith, Adam   39
  Sydney   59
  William   40

Smythe, Percy Clinton Sydney *see* Strangford, viscount
Somerset, Henry *see* Beaufort, duke of
Sondes, George John Milles, 4th baron   89
Spencer, George John, 2nd earl   36
    John Charles *see* Althorp, viscount
Spofforth, Markham   89, 90
Spring Rice, Thomas *see* Monteagle, baron
Stanley, 2nd baron *see* Derby, 14th earl of
    Edward Geoffrey *see* Derby, 14th earl of
    Edward Henry *see* Derby, 15th earl of
Stephen, James   40
Stewart, Dugald   59
Strangford, Percy Clinton Sydney Smythe, 6th viscount [I]   49
Sydney, Thomas Townshend, 1st viscount   29, 30

Taylor, Thomas Edward   90
Teignmouth, John Shore, 1st baron [I]   35
Temple, Henry John *see* Palmerston, viscount
Thatcher, Margaret   75
Thornton, Henry   41
Thurlow, Edward, 1st baron, chancellor   30, 35
Thynne, John Alexander *see* Bath, 4th marquess of
    Thomas *see* Bath, 2nd marquess of
Tierney, George   37, 58, 61
Townshend, George *see* Leicester, earl of
    Thomas *see* Sydney, viscount
Tufnell, Henry   72

Vescy-Fitzgerald, William *see* Fitzgerald, baron
Vesey, John *see* De Vesci, viscount

Victoria, queen   72
Villiers, George William Frederick *see* Clarendon, earl of

Walpole, Horace   19
Warwick, George Greville, 2nd earl of   33
    Henry Richard Greville, 3rd earl of   83
Watson-Wentworth, Charles *see* Rockingham, marquess of
Wedderburn, Alexander see Loughborough, baron
Wellesley, Richard, marquess [I]   39, 43
Wellington, Arthur Wellesley, 1st duke of   1–7, 9–11, 43–55, 72, 76, 82
West, George John *see* De la Warr, earl
Westmorland, John Fane, 10th earl of   41, 49
Wilberforce, Willaim   40, 42
William IV, king, previously duke of Clarence   4, 33, 41, 42, 48
Winchilsea, George William Finch-Hatton, 10th earl of   50
Windham, William   32, 33
Wingfield, Mervyn *see* Powerscourt, viscount
Wodehouse, John, 3rd baron   68, 69, 83
Wyndahm, William *see* Grenville, baron
Wyndham-Quin, Windham Henry *see* Dunraven, earl of

York, archbishop of *see* Maclagan, William Dalrymple
York, duke of *see* Edward Augustus, prince